Day Camp from Day One

A Hands-on Guide
for Day Camp Administrators

Connie Coutellier

American Camping Association®

Cover design: Joyce Koeper

Editorial services and text design: Janice M. Phelps

Front cover photo credits: Clockwise, ACA file photo; The Fowler Center;
Catalina Island Camp; ACA file photo; YMCA Benjamin Harrison Day
Camp; Bryce Hunt, Photographer, © Girls Scouts Limberlost Council
2002; Center, Camp Tall Turf

American Camping Association, Inc.
5000 State Road 67 North
Martinsville, Indiana 46151-7902
765-342-8456
800-428-CAMP
www.ACAcamps.org

ISBN 0-87603-187-4

A CIP catalog record for this book can be obtained
from the Library of Congress.

Table of Contents

Chapter 7: Keeping Your Campers Safe . . . and Your Camp Protected—Risk Management and Crisis Communication

Chapter 8: Looking Ahead to Your Future Success

Introduction

"When all is said and done, people of all ages want to be part of something bigger and more important than themselves. More than anything else, this is the value that camp teaches kids. It offers them a sense of perspective and provides them with a head start on the road to becoming truly human . . . And that is why all of you should be so proud of what you do."
–Mr. Michael Eisner, CEO, The Walt Disney Company
Excerpted from a speech delivered at the 2001 Tri-State Camping Conference
Used by permission from Disney Enterprises, Inc.

Perhaps it came as an e-mail that flashed across your screen one morning: "Good news! We've found the funding for a two-week art day camp for six- to eight-year-olds. This is just the kind of program that the community wants and needs. We know with your energy, background and determination you can make this a huge success. Interested?"

You sit back. Of course you're interested. For someone with your interests and background, starting and running a day camp, after all, falls in the category of "dream job."

Perhaps you've already worked on the sidelines and seen first-hand the positive effect the camp experience can have on enriching the lives of children. Perhaps it was as a Sunday school teacher, staff member in a community center, or volunteer in Boy or Girl Scouts where you learned how important an organized camp experience is to a child's development. Or maybe you're just interested in using your talents and those of others in your community to bring important life skills to the young people of your area.

Whatever your background, if you're reading this book chances are *you know the transforming power that organized camp activities can play in the lives of those they serve.*

Whether you'll be managing an existing day camp, or beginning a new one, you recognize this opportunity for what it is: your chance to use your skills and background to positively contribute to the lives of others. But wait . . . You click off a quick inventory of the knowledge and skills you think you might need to make your first foray in day camp administration a success. Some skills you're confident you have. Others . . . well, you're not so sure.

"Sure, I've worked with kids . . . I've developed activities, even programs. But I've never planned or run a camp before. I can imagine the amount of preparation and work that goes into this kind of thing . . . Am I up to it? How do I go about it? Where do I start?"

Take a deep breath. You start where you are: with this book.

Remember, there's not a person who's run a successful day camp program who *hasn't* asked *"Where do I start?"* at one time or another. Now, the sooner you get down to work finding an effective strategy for hitting the ground running as a day camp administrator, the sooner you can begin the important work of delivering the kind of camp program that changes lives.

Getting the answers to your questions about day camp administration is what this book is all about. You will gain the information, understanding, tools, and best practices you'll need for planning and running a dynamic and effective day camp from day one—*and keeping it successful.*

The management of day camps requires skill, vision and effective and innovative short- and long-range strategies. Seasoned day camp administrators know that while proven expertise in a range of camp-related disciplines may help an individual in his or her first work in day camp administration, *the planning or running of a day camp is itself a specialized and many-faceted undertaking.*

Experienced administrators know that running a day camp requires a sound understanding of many elements, including business and marketing, interpersonal dynamics, and regulatory requirements, among many others. They also know that for the beginner the path forward can lie through a craggy and confusing landscape, one abounding in more navigational challenges than the roughest camp hike.

This book is designed to serve as an easy-to-follow, informative roadmap through the challenging terrain that can be your first administrative day camp experience. It offers the guidance you'll need to develop the kind of organized, well-informed and unified approach to day camp planning and administration that is key to successful camp programs. In addition, the book brings together a wide body of information designed to give you a good up-front understanding and mastery of the many elements of a day camp program.

In addition to providing a general overview of planning and running a camp, this guide will offer "deep dives" into the key areas of camp administration. While not intended to provide the definitive or last word on running a day camp, the book is designed to give the reader a thorough and comprehensive introduction to—and orientation in—day camp administration.

The book is organized sequentially to provide a systematic, step-by-step overview of all elements involved in launching and running a day camp. A fictional camp, "Camp ARTastic" appears throughout the text as a working model to illustrate some of the concepts discussed in the book.

The book ranges across all key facets of camp administration—from establishing a mission or purpose, goals and desired youth development outcomes for your camp, to satisfying legal and regulatory requirements, to leveraging principles of continuous improvement to ensure on-going success for your camp once it's up-and-running.

Also, accompanying the book is a CD-ROM containing sample forms, checklists and other tools referenced throughout the book. These tools, which are easily customized for use with your program, are designed to give you a quick and easy way to ensure that key areas of your camp administration are adequately planned, organized and documented.

I wish to express my thanks to the camp professionals who gave generously of their time to help with this project: Jeff Ackerman, DD Gass, Joe Long, Jennifer Naylor, Sandra Thompson and Chris Winkler. I would especially like to thank Nick Crews for his great ideas and questions, terrific interviewing skills, and his continual support and dedication.

I offer this book to the camp community with the hope that it helps those new to the day camp director experience—as well as those more experienced—to successfully navigate the details and requirements of day camp administration with the view of delivering effective, life-changing programs.

Connie Coutellier
Monrovia, Indiana
2003

© *Girl Scouts of Limberlost Council, 2002/Bryce Hunt*

Chapter 1

Hit the Ground Running with a Good Foundation

"If you don't know where you're going, how will you know when you get there?"

You've always dreamed of directing your own day camp. Or perhaps you've been asked to direct your organization's day camp, or start a new camp. After indicating to the camp board that you know *nothing* about running a day camp ("You'll do wonderfully," they've assured you), you've taken the job. Not without some trepidation, mind you; after all, who knows your lack of administrative experience in this area better than you?

Sure, you've always been a quick study. But even a flitting look at the vast informational resources on day camp administration, available online for instance, is as daunting as it is overwhelming. So, you're going to start a day camp. Now what? Where do you start?

A word of advice from an experienced day camp director is a good place to start. Jeff Ackerman, director of the Elmwood Country Day Camp in Westchester, New York for seventeen years, underscores the need for good planning in a day camp operation.

"The basics [in day camp administration] have to be done absolutely perfectly so that you're free to do the more important developmental work. We could be running the greatest swim program in the world, but if our bus driver is not safety conscious, it doesn't matter. The details are enormous. From grouping of kids, to matching staff with kids, to making sure everybody has a medical form in . . . "

Attention to detail, says, Ackerman, is everything. "Running a day camp is like putting together a 1,500-piece jigsaw puzzle; you've got to get every piece in, otherwise it's not going to work."

Thorough planning is the foundation to a successful day camp program. Before you can *do* successfully, you must *plan* successfully. The most creative vision for a camp, the best staff, the most innovative and engaging activities—these won't get you very far without good front-end planning and well-laid groundwork. This is the common element to every successful program.

To put it another way: Knowing where you're going, is a good first step in ensuring you'll get there.

Any gifted architect acknowledges the role inspiration plays in a great design. But he or she also knows that a good foundation, not just creative vision, plays the most significant role in the overall success of an architectural achievement.

The same is true for day camps. Your ability to accomplish your goals and outcomes exist in direct relationship to the foundation you lay for the successful management of the details of your day-to-day operation. Good planning is basic to a successful program.

"Why are we doing this?"

As a new camp director, you must first consider *why* your organization or community wants a day camp. As anyone who has seriously grappled with this question will tell you, this exercise is not a no-brainer, as it might at first appear.

Before we consider the "why" behind your camp, it is useful to review day camp types with a view to determining what model best reflects your situation.

Camp types

The American Camping Association (ACA) defines camp as: "*A sustained experience which provides a creative, recreational, and educational opportunity in group living in the outdoors. It utilizes trained leadership and the resources of the natural surroundings to contribute to each camper's mental, physical, social, and spiritual growth.*"

Day camps, as the name suggests, are generally daytime-based programs. In their excellent overview of camp types, Armand and Beverly Ball define day camps as those that "operate only during a portion of the day, typically morning and afternoon, usually for five successive days of the week, Monday through Friday. However there are day camps which operate only three days a week, others which operate in the evening hours, and many which include at least one overnight experience . . . " [1]

In recent years, day camps that offer extended day options have become increasingly popular. This has been driven in part by the need for additional hours of childcare. These extended programs, many of which exist as programs that are independent from the central camp program, provide a much-needed community service for parents with childcare needs, especially in the summer months.

An important structural consideration that will determine your administrative set-up is whether your camp will be a not-for-profit or for-profit operation. Because each designation calls for a specific and differing set of administrative guidelines (to be discussed in Chapter 5), it's important to understand the difference between a not-for-profit and for-profit camp. As Armand and Beverly Ball write, "The for-profit camp or entrepreneurial camp may be operated by an individual, partners, or a corporation to return a profit to the owner, including some return on capital investment made in property and facilities . . .

"The not-for-profit camp may be owned by an organization . . . Public camps are those operated by a government body, such as a parks-and-recreation department . . . Funding comes from fees and tax dollars. They may be owned by a private tax-exempt corporation or foundation. In all of these cases, the camp has a tax exemption under article 501 (c) (3) of the federal tax code or is operated by a governmental body . . . " [2]

Underlying the legal definition of a not-for-profit camp is the implied goal of advancing the welfare of society—not making a profit. The not-for-profit camp must carefully adhere to the organization's mission and conduct its business without violating ethical standards. For example, the Internal Revenue Service regulations that govern not-for-profit organizations state that managerial staff, members of the board of trustees and others that have decision-making responsibilities may be held liable for financial errors of which they were, or should have been, aware. Such violations may also jeopardize their 501 (c) (3) tax-exempt status.

Perhaps your new camp is rooted in an identified or perceived community need. Or maybe it is simply an outgrowth of your personal camp vision. Maybe your idea for a new camp simply derives from an interest in pursing a business opportunity. Whatever the reason, a critical first step in your new job is becoming familiar with the underlying reasons driving the need for your camp. To do this, you'll need to begin by asking—and answering—the question *Why are we doing this?*

Even if you have not had direct input into the decision to start a day camp, good planning from now on requires that you clearly understand the purpose or mission of your camp. So let's start with exploring the "why" behind this endeavor.

To begin uncovering your camp's purposes, you'll need to ask several questions, among them:

- Who has made the decision to have a day camp?
- What was the reason?
- Does your organization have a mission? What is it?
- Will this day camp contribute to this mission?
- How will a camper benefit from this day camp?
- What things can this day camp provide that parents want for their children?

Has a community needs assessment indicated a need for a camp? Is there a need for summer programming in your community? Is a day camp the best way to meet this need? Are there other programs in the community that will be competing for the same resources, target population, or participants?

And then there is the most important question of all: How will your day camp contribute to the mission of your sponsoring organization? If you're starting your own camp, ask, "What is my personal mission or goal?"

Taken together, the answers to these questions can give you the information you'll need to identify the reason for launching or continuing a camp.

These are only a few of the many questions that you will face in your early program planning. Don't panic. A systematic approach to defining and articulating a purpose for your camp will enable you to sift through the welter of information to arrive at a well-defined camp mission.

If you'll be running an existing day camp, chances are that the question, "Why a day camp?" has already been answered for you. If you'll be developing a program for a new camp, this will be the question that will fundamentally shape and define all that you will do from here on out. For this reason, it is essential that as the new director you make your first order of business understanding—and documenting—the "whys" behind your new camp.

For the existing camp

For the new director of an existing camp, beginning to understand the "whys" can be as easy as reviewing existing brochures, marketing, or Web-based resources, or meeting with a camp committee, board, supervisor, or owner to review your camp's goals and mission. At this point a good rule-of-thumb comes into play: "Do your homework."

Often, this process to understand a camp's background begins for the new director before he or she has even gotten the job; for instance, as research done in

Courtesy of Camp Laurel, Lebanon, Connecticut

preparation for an employment interview. Yet, getting the job doesn't mean your assessment ends. In fact, your understanding of the role your camp will play within an organization or community may be an ever-changing work-in-progress; one that will require frequent reevaluations throughout the course of your camp's operation. For now, however, it's important to get a snap-shot of what specific services and deliverables your camp will bring to your organization or community.

The better up-front understanding you have of your camp's "reason for being," the better you'll be prepared to address the details and specific challenges of actual camp administration. And the easier it will to plan and put together a successful program—one that solidly serves organizational or personal aims and, most important, brings a range of benefits to your campers.

If you are a new director of an *existing* camp, keep in mind that the philosophy and intent of your sponsoring organization or owner, *not* your personal vision, must define the overall purpose of your camp. A strong personal commitment is almost always viewed as a valued asset in any camp director. Be that as it may, your personal "camp vision" should not in any way distract you from fulfilling your all-important responsibility of running a camp that *clearly reflects your organization's purpose or mission for its camp.*

Identifying a purpose for the new camp

If you've been charged with starting a new day camp, you may have to dig a little deeper to really understand what role or purpose your camp will serve.

There are as many reasons a community needs a camp as there are camps, or even communities. The organization (or individual) that has asked you to develop and run the new camp probably has at least some general understanding of "why" this camp ought to exist. As the new director, however, you'll need to thoroughly define, point-by-point, the specific deliverables your camp will provide to your sponsoring organization or owner and the community. Once you've done this, you'll also need to clearly articulate your findings to your supervisor or the group—for instance, a camp committee or organizational board of directors—who will be overseeing your camp. It is important that your stakeholders, or those who'll be backing your operation, know that you clearly understand your community and the needs that your camp will address.

Most important, this knowledge will enable you to plan and bring to life a program that is well-targeted to the needs of those it will serve: a key advantage as you work later to successfully market your program.

Defining a mission and purpose for your camp

Understanding your camp's mission and purpose—and the desired outcomes, or program goals—is a key part of your planning process. A critical first step in developing an action plan is to define what end-objective your camp will serve. Your mission and purpose is different than the more general question, "Why does my camp exist?" Answering the question "Why do we need a camp?" helps you uncover the context—organizational or community—in which your camp will be operating, and gives you a general understanding of the needs your camp will be fulfilling.

If you'll be joining the staff of an existing camp as camp director, the organization's or camp's mission and purpose is probably already clearly articulated and thoroughly integrated into the camp's culture. In cases where a mission or purpose has not been formally established, a group's vision or mission statement, or other organizational charter, often provides some indication of the kind of camp you'll be expected to run or put together. Whatever the case, one of your first duties as new camp director should be to systematically review pertinent information with a view toward understanding the real or implied mission and purpose of your organization or the camp.

Understanding the mission brings several important benefits to your camp-planning process. First, it solidly links the overall purpose of your camp to any organizational charter or goals of the sponsoring or backing group. Then, it can help you evaluate the camp's contribution to the mission and to its operational realities.

Determining a mission statement: a how-to

If you're joining an existing camp that has no formal mission statement, developing one can be an excellent way to ensure that the camp under your leadership is aligned with the appropriate organizational goals. For the moment, you can set aside the many details of camp planning to focus on clearly and succinctly defining the essential reason your camp exists.

If your camp is simply an outgrowth of your personal vision, a mission statement gives you the chance to clearly think through and articulate what you want to achieve. It's also a good way to chart your way forward.

A mission statement is:

- by its very nature theoretical and difficult to measure,
- the essential reason for the existence of a camp,
- clear and concise,
- something that others can remember and to which they can relate, and
- reviewed occasionally, but not changed very often.

Let's look at a few examples of mission statements. The first three might be that of an organization and the second three appropriate for a camp that may not have a parent organization.

- To provide support and recreation for families from diverse backgrounds in the metropolitan area.
- To create opportunities for individuals to explore and deepen their religious and spiritual beliefs.
- To offer activities and health education for individuals with chronic illnesses and their families.
- To provide positive lifestyle alternative for adjudicated youth through wilderness challenge programs.
- To help young people develop life skills utilizing an outdoor environment.
- To promote individual skill development and personal fitness through athletic competition.

Now take a few minutes and try to write your organization's mission. Can you remember it? Does it give your camp direction? Can you visualize how your camp might contribute to the mission?

Developing a camp that develops campers: youth development

Identifying your mission and purpose enables you to *specifically* define the desired youth development outcomes or benefits of the camp experience. These are the benefits that your camp promises parents it will contribute to the development of their child.

Parents want the best opportunities for their children. They want their children to have whatever it takes to be happy and successful—good health, ability to get along with others, thinking and problem-solving skills, and a good self-concept. Youth development experts agree that children need resiliency skills: self-esteem, life skills, self-reliance and pro-social behaviors. The camp experience offers a nurturing environment away from the distractions and, in some cases, hostile environment of the city, to acquire these skills.

Youth development experts recognize the value that a positive camp experience can provide. Dr. Peter Scales, senior fellow at The Search Institute says, "The biggest plus of camp is that camps help young people discover and explore their talents, interests, and values. Kids who have had these kinds of [camp] experiences end up being healthier and have less problems which concern us all."

Press Release on the Research Project Oct. 29, 2001[3]

The National Collaboration for Youth (NCY), representing thirty-nine of the leading national youth development organizations in the United States, works to provide a united voice for all youth, advocating for improved conditions and opportunities for their positive development.

NYC defines youth development as a process that prepares young people to meet the challenges of adolescence and adulthood through a coordinated, progressive series of activities and experiences which help make them socially, morally, emotionally, physically and cognitively competent.

The National Youth Development Information Center is a project of the NCY dedicated to assisting educators and others who work with young people in helping youth develop core competencies and assets. Additional resources on youth development can be found on their Web page www.nydic.org/nydic/index.html.

One of the greatest challenges in youth development is clearly identifying how schools, youth-serving agencies, camps, and others can each play an effective, complementary role in helping young people on their journey to productive adulthood. Positive youth development is an interrelated process that involves all of the influencers in a child's life working together to build resilience to the stresses and challenges encountered in the everyday world.

Camp activities and group living in a natural environment are the tools used to create camp communities. These communities promote successful, healthy development and offer a place where fun is a daily goal. In this type of structured environment, children interact with positive role models who have time to listen, talk, relax, and reflect. They learn to work together, make choices, take responsibility, develop creative skills, build independence and self-reliance, and gain confidence. All are necessary steps on a child's path to a healthy, productive life.

But how do you identify the specific areas of development that you need to plan your program around? First by arriving at your outcomes.

Determining your outcomes

Once you've determined your camp's mission and purpose and have a basic understanding of youth development, arriving at a set of specific outcomes should be relatively easy. Outcomes are identified "improvement areas" in competency and skills that you seek, through your program, to bring about in campers. Outcomes are benefits that camp participants experience during and after the camp program. Outcomes may relate to knowledge, skills, attitudes, values, behaviors, conditions or status. Taken together, these outcomes define the scope and specifics of how campers will be positively changed as a result of their camp experience. They define how you will contribute to the mission.

Figure 1.1 shows sample outcomes. Use the template on the CD to list your outcomes and rank them by importance. List the specific competency and skill areas you are targeting; remember to "lead with a verb," that is, begin each listing with an action word that illustrates how the camper will actually change, or

Outcomes are everything . . .

Your program outcomes — sometimes called "objectives" — should inform and shape all facets of administrative and program development at every step of your planning. Every aspect of your camp's program — from how you teach swimming, to how you transport, and even feed your campers should solidly support the outcomes you develop for your camp.

Before adopting any program or administrative solution to your program ask, "Does this support our outcomes?" If an element of your program does not support your outcomes, replace it with something that does.

benefit, from the camp experience. Don't forget, concepts are nothing without the action needed to bring them about.

Outcomes

Figure 1.1

Outcomes are benefits to participants during and after the program. That is, how will the campers be changed as a result of being at day camp?

As a result of my day camp, campers will:	Rank
Increase their ability to work with others	1
Demonstrate a growing ability to make decisions	5
Show increased self confidence	2
Increase eagerness to try new things or develop new skills	4
Build awareness and ability to follow basic health and safety rules	3

Choosing the site to support outcomes

In addition to formalizing the more program-related aspects of your camp, you'll need to find just the right spot your new camp can call "home." If your camp already is established in its "digs," this section might be of less interest than it will be to someone charged with the task of finding a site for a new camp. But if you need to find just *the right* place for your new camp, listen up. The following exercises can help.

Outcomes drive activities. For this reason, your camp type and activity mix will, of course, largely determine your camp setting. For example, a camp having an outcome of increased awareness of the natural environment would have to be extremely creative to accomplish this aim in the middle of a paved inner-city playground.

An effective way to approach the site selection process is to revisit much of the information you've already assembled about your camp, and put it through a series of exercises tailored to help you establish specific site requirements for your camp.

Figure 1.2 provides a framework for assigning and ranking values for specific site features. Once you have completed it, you can use it as a guide while touring sites.

Site Selection Ranking Checklist

Rank by importance to operating your day camp

1 = a must   2 = would be nice   3 = could do without

Figure 1.2

Rank

Site Selection

_____ Access to wooded areas or the natural environment
_____ Municipally owned park
_____ Large indoor shelter for program and safety
_____ Shelter or program space for small groups
_____ Large, flat outdoor space
_____ Places for building fires or cooking outdoors
_____ Security and/or privacy
_____ Access to swimming
_____ Access to water for fishing or boating
_____ Picnic tables or group space
_____ Storage space available: lockable, safe
_____ First-aid building or shelter
_____ Office space available
_____ Telephone service available
_____ Preferred dates available
_____ Free or very reasonable cost
_____ Approved drinking water
_____ Hot water
_____ Toddler area for volunteer staff's children
_____ Program area for target sports or other specialty activities
_____ Area for arts and crafts with water and electricity
_____ Accessible bathrooms
_____ Weather shelter
_____ Storm shelter
_____ What other groups might be using the space—are you compatible?
_____ Convenient location for your target population
_____ Other:_____

Transportation

_____ Access to public transportation
_____ Within a reasonable distance for daily transportation
_____ Daily transportation
_____ Camp plans to rent or buy vehicles
_____ Camp already owns vehicles
_____ Camp expects parents or volunteers to provide transportation
_____ Ease of supervision during transportation
_____ Parking areas adequate space at peak times
_____ Safe loading and unloading areas
_____ Accessibility for field trips
_____ Other:_____

continued on next page...

Figure 1.2

Food Service

_____ Places where cookouts could be part of the program
_____ Campers bring sack lunches and may need coolers for drinks
_____ Facility for serving hot meals
_____ Cold storage for drinks and perishable foods
_____ Hot water
_____ Community-sponsored meals
_____ Refrigerator/freezer
_____ Rodent-free storage for supplies
_____ Stove/microwave
_____ Dishwasher
_____ Dish cleaning areas

Touring a site

Whether you are selecting a new site or looking at how you will use your organization's existing facilities for the day camp, site tours give you an excellent opportunity to uncover the assets—and identify potential problems—of a proposed day camp site.

As you inspect a potential site, do so with the eyes of an administer. First, begin with a general inspection. Review your completed Site Selection Ranking Checklist. Does the site generally conform to the requirements of your camp? Are there features of the site under review that make it inappropriate for use for your camp?

After the site under consideration has passed a general inspection, take your evaluation of the site to the next level by checking some important specifics:

- Check to see if the appropriate local and state permits and licenses are available or can be obtained for this property. These will vary by state, county, and local municipality.
- Determine whether the sanitation system for bathrooms is approved and appropriate for the number of participants and staff you intend to have. ACA standards suggest a minimum of one toilet seat for every thirty females and one for every fifty males. Are there adjacent hand-washing facilities? You may need to check your state laws for specific guidelines on hand-washing requirements.
- Review the site for health and safety factors. Are there natural or manmade hazards such as cliffs, water, or holes? Are there busy streets running adjacent to or through the property? Is the site well-maintained?
- Look at the layout of the property; consider how the site will complement your overall program. Would the site or its setting require changes or adaptations to your program?

- Check the location. Is it convenient for transportation, medical help or emergency services? Is the area considered safe? How easy would it be to control access points?
- Survey the camp's immediate neighborhood. Do the homes or activities surrounding the property create potential problems? If you are planning to buy, what are the future plans for the area?
- If it is not your property, be sure there is agreement on responsibility for maintenance of building and grounds, cleaning and trash removal.
- If you are renting the site, consider having the contract checked by an attorney. If the site is currently used as a camp, determine if it is accredited by the American Camping Association.
- Evaluate how the site will accommodate planned program activities, assist with meeting program outcomes, and fulfill safety requirements.

The sample matrix in Figure 1.3 shows how one might evaluate a prospective site against a specific set of program requirements. You will find a copy of this matrix on the CD for your use in evaluating a prospective site.

Prospective Site Matrix

List your activities	Can it be done on on this site?	Does it contribute to the program outcomes?	Does it meet safety requirements?
Swimming	Yes: pool	Yes	Yes: large area of shallow water
Flag raising	No: existing pole	Yes	n/a
Arts and crafts	Yes: shelter	Yes	Yes: no running water
Nature activities	Yes: small	Yes	No: no trails, natural area lots of poison ivy
Outdoor cooking	Yes: only one large grill	No	No: not age-appropriate
Field sports	Yes	Yes	Yes: large level

Figure 1.3

Site selection by SWOT

A SWOT analysis (short for "Strengths, Weaknesses, Opportunities and Threats") offers another way to diagram the relative merits of a prospective site. Figure 1.4 shows a sample.

SWOT Analysis

Figure 1.4

Strengths: What are the strengths, or advantages, of this day camp site? What makes it special?

Weaknesses: What are the weaknesses, or bad points, of this site? What would I prefer was not there?

Opportunities: Look at the list of strengths and weaknesses, and ask: what opportunities might they open up for you on this site?

Threats: What threats might weaken your business or what obstacles will this site create for you?

If I choose this site how can I overcome the weaknesses and threats?

Strengths
+ pool with shallow area and changing area
+ large shelter and storage for crafts
+ small shelter for administration and first aid
+ convenient for target population
+ large grassy area for sports
+ can be rented for private use
+ picnic tables for each group
+ available on dates desired

Weaknesses
- no large flag pole
- no place for cooking out
- no parking area for buses
- no storage for administrative supplies
- no water in shelter area

Opportunities
+ swimming lessons
+ large field area for all-camp programs
+ church across the street with large parking lot
+ movement between activities short

Threats
- poison ivy
- danger crossing street
- easy public access

For example, given the SWOT analysis, you might consider:

✓ using the camp van to store administrative supplies each day;
✓ having a flag ceremony using a hand-held flag pole;
✓ asking a site manager to fill and deliver water containers for the shelter area;
✓ establishing safety procedures for crossing the street; and
✓ informing authorities about your specific use of the site and dates of use (train staff to question strangers).

If I choose this site, how can I take advantage of the strengths and opportunities?
For example given the SWOT analysis, you might consider:

✓ using a large storage area in the craft shelter to store group boxes at end of each day;
✓ asking the church for permission to load and unload buses on its lot;
✓ planning an all-day specially themed camp event for Wednesday that uses the field;
✓ offering special options for children who wish swimming lessons at the close of the regular day; and
✓ assigning each group a picnic table "home" and storage box for their use during the week.

A SWOT analysis is an excellent way to determine if the strengths and opportunities outweigh the weaknesses and threats. It can also help the "thinking through" process you'll need to overcome any potential problems. If nothing else, a SWOT analysis is a good discussion starter. One that will help you to look objectively at your strengths, analyze the weaknesses and take advantage of opportunities available and address any threats.

Finding your camp's "Home Sweet Home"

As these exercises suggest, it might take a bit of rigorous evaluation before your camp finds its "home sweet home." However, as anyone who has tried to run a camp in a less-than-appropriate setting will tell you, going the extra mile to find the *right* site for your camp is well worth the effort.

Your camp's site is one of the most significant factors, not only in its "look and feel," but its ability to deliver on your outcomes. Your home reflects who you are, and exists to fulfill your specific individual needs; really, the same is true for your camp's site as it relates to your program.

Your camp's site is an important enabler of your program; do the necessary work to find the site that's right for you.

Welcome to Camp ARTastic

Mary Michaels has accepted an invitation by the board of Union City Art League to head up the group's two-week art day camp for six- to eight-year-olds.

Mary's initial excitement at the prospect of putting together "the day camp of her dreams" is now being rapidly replaced by the low-level panic over the amount of work there is to be done. At times like these, however, Mary does not get too anxious: she chooses instead to get *focused and organized.*

As a starting point, Mary sits down and, pen in hand, starts mapping out the kind of camp she *thinks* she's been asked to run. A meeting with the camp committee has done much to clarify what the underlying focus of her program will be: essentially, to increase interest in art, give children an opportunity for creative expression and build confidence.

Fortunately for Mary, many of the operational aspects of her camp have already been determined by the committee and art league. For instance, the group has already selected a site for the camp.

As an exercise to help her better understand the purpose of the day camp, however, she answers the questions listed at the beginning of this chapter:

- "Who has made the decision to have a day camp?"
  That one's easy: the camp committee.
- "What is the reason for the camp?"
  To offer art-related education to children in the specified age group, build confidence and related social skills.
- "Does your organization have a mission?"
  Yes, the art league's mission is to help individuals bring to their lives the enrichment that comes with developing skills in the fine arts.
- "Will this day camp contribute to this mission?"
  Yes, (or at least Mary hopes so!)
- "How will a camper benefit from being in this day camp?"
  In addition to gaining hands-on experience in the mechanics of the fine arts, the camp will support the campers in achieving a broad range of social and other skills and personal development.
- "What do you think parents want this day camp to give their child?"
  A safe, fun and supportive environment that encourages a wide range of personal development.

It helps that Mary has done her homework. She has already met with members of her newly formed camp committee and other art league members; it has made her job easier that these individuals have clearly communicated what they see as the purpose, mission, and needed outcomes for the camp.

Mary then decides to create a purpose statement for her camp that will contribute to the mission statement of the art league: "ARTastic Day Camp provides a safe and supportive environment that promotes excitement about developing skills in the arts."

After she drafts her statement, Mary reviews it with the camp committee, which approves it. Finally, she compiles a list of "outcomes" that will serve as the key goals for her camp program:

As a result of my day camp, campers will:

	Rank
✓ gain ability in using different art media for creative expression,	1
✓ increase their enjoyment and understanding of basic art concepts,	2
✓ show improved willingness to share with others, and	3
✓ use materials safely and respectfully.	4

Moving forward from a basis of good ground work

Beginning the task of starting or continuing a day camp requires a methodical and systematic approach to some of the early challenges. There is much that lies ahead; for now, however, congratulate yourself on your new-found ability to lay the groundwork of identifying your program's need, purpose, and mission, and carrying the process through to identification of your core outcomes.

[Notes]

1. Armand & Beverly Ball, 2000. *Basic Camp Management:* American Camping Association. p. 5

2. Ibid. p. 6

3. Press Release on the Research Project Oct. 29, 2001

Courtesy of Crystal Lake Park District, Crystal Lake, Illinois

Chapter 2

Your Camp as Community

Day camp gives young people the unique experience of gaining life-skills in a small and supportive community, one that's squarely based on the goal of helping them realize their maximum potential through participation in a structured camp program.

Unlike resident camps that may be far from the camper's home, day camps are normally based in a local community; they are, in fact, "communities within a community." Much like school children, day campers often interact with family and neighborhood at the close of each day. The day camper may also be younger than the typical resident camper, and not interested, or ready, to be away from home overnight.

Because residential camps can be beyond the means of many families, the day camp experience may be one of the few developmental opportunities, or supportive communities, some young people will enjoy. For this reason, it is imperative that those who plan and run day camps understand the important role that the camp community plays in the success of a program.

In many ways, the success of the overall camp experience exists in direct proportion to the strength and cohesiveness of a camp community. In general, a camp shares similarities with other traditional community models, such as family and church/temple. Yet a camp provides a unique experience. As Armand and Beverly Ball point out, "The camp community is interdependent and to some degree isolated from the outside . . . Building on the sense of community [that a camp offers] can have great educational benefits, as well as develop the sort of relationships and loyalty that endures for many years." [1]

Like any strong community, day camp is first and foremost a supportive environment. It is also a necessary prerequisite to the educational and developmental process. Of course, good activities that support your overall outcomes are key. But activities and other program elements are secondary to the central need for a strong camp community having a quality staff that understands and supports that community. After all, your camp community serves as the *overall context* for all that you do. This being the case, it is important to make establishing a rich and supportive community a key focus of your camp planning.

Community and youth development

What kind of communities best foster youth development? Youth development experts and current research suggest that several factors improve the likelihood that young people will reach their potential and become successful and productive citizens. These include access to communities that provide supportive relationships, safe and caring environments, structure, and opportunities for meaningful involvement. Supportive factors also include availability of challenging and engaging activities and learning experiences. But how do you build this type of community?

First, let's look at the campers who will make up that community.

Who are your campers?

You've identified your camp's purpose, mission and outcomes. The next step in the planning process is to determine *who* your campers will be. Nothing should inform the "look, feel and purpose" of your camp more than the needs of those who will be served by it.

To begin, take a general look at the community your camp will serve. Ask: Who is my target population [i.e. your campers]? Follow-up with some preliminary questions: Within this group is there a perceived need for a camp such as this? Will this community agree with, or see the value in, this camp's mission, or that of its backing organization?

Before you go further in the planning process, take a close look at your target population. Try to get an accurate assessment of its needs and interests. At this juncture, you should learn everything you can about the specific needs of your target population. You must also determine your operational parameters, for instance, the ages of the campers you wish to serve and the number of campers the program will accommodate.

Outlining your community/camp/camper profile

Conducting an environmental scan or developing a community/camp/camper profile is a good way to get an initial snapshot of the camper you should be targeting. Begin by working through a process to help define a profile of your community and identify the kind of camper you'll want to target. Some of the questions below will be easier to answer as you move through this chapter and the rest of the book. However a quick review of them now will help you in the current task of identifying your target population.

A typical exercise might look like this:

- What are the three top needs this community has for a day camp?
- Will your camp's mission, purpose and outcomes fulfill these needs?
- Will the planned setting of the camp support your outcomes?
- What sort of activities will best support your outcomes? Are these activities aligned with the needs and interest of the community?
- Will your day camp primarily serve children who will walk to the site or whose parents drop them off? If not, what will be specific transportation needs? If your transportation route requires multiple stops, try to limit the time children spend on a bus or van to no longer than one hour; this may help you map out your area.
- List any competing camp programs in the area. What are the major organizational and program attributes of these camps? Is there a competitive edge that your camp can achieve by delivering a program better targeted to the wants and needs of the community? What are the ways your camp will better meet those community needs? (Note: Any competitive advantage can become a key point of marketing leverage that you'll want to incorporate in your marketing plan. (This will be discussed more fully in Chapter 6.)
- Does your organization have members, or provide other services, in the area you're targeting?
- Do you plan to serve only boys, only girls, or have a coed camp?
- What are the income levels and other economic factors that your camp might need to consider?
- What kind of community support is available to your camp?
- How many children are from single-parent families? How many are from families with both parents employed outside the home?
- Is there a need for an extended camp program, or to address other child-care-related needs?
- What is the demographic profile of your potential campers? Are there cultural identity-related factors to consider?

ACA file photo

Informational resources from the U.S. government can greatly assist you in understanding the demographics of your potential campers, and planning your program to meet those needs.

To access this information, visit the following Web site:

www.factfinder.census.gov/servlet/BasicFactsServlet

Under "Basic Facts for Housing and Population" select (the city or town, county, and so on) of your targeted area. Define the state, county, city, and other information that the site requests. The information the site will give you will provide a demographic breakdown in that area by age, race and general housing-related information.

The information that you collect through this exercise will help you better target your camper population and ensure a closer alignment of your program to their needs.

If your organization is already serving this population, or area, you may only need to reacquaint yourself with the information, with a view toward deciding if you'll need to expand your camp's scope, or change the age group you'll serve. This information will also help you better understand your potential market and determine if you have enough children in the area to successfully operate a camp.

Your camper profile: age

Once you gain a general understanding of the demographic landscape of the area your camp will be serving, you'll want to focus specifically on clarifying what ages you'll be targeting.

Because developmental approaches vary widely depending on the age group, age is an important consideration in planning day camp programs. Age grouping plays a key role in determining the kind of activities and programs you'll need to meet the needs of the potential camper and achieve your outcomes. For this reason, identifying the ages of the campers you'll serve is an important part of your planning process.

As you begin to work through steps to determine your target age groups, you may find it useful to revisit your community/camp/camper profile. With your overall profile in mind, now ask:

- Given the demographic profile we've developed, what ages have the greatest need for a day camp?
- Are my outcomes appropriate for the age groups we've identified?
- Will my camp enable campers in the identified age group to achieve developmental and other successes outlined in my outcomes?
- Will my identified age group require special needs that might impact my budget or other resources?

Let's check in with Mary over at Camp ARTastic and see how she's progressing with her camp planning.

After collecting all the information she can find about her community, Mary makes some informed decisions about identifying her target population. Now she begins collecting names for a database of potential target families.

Many of these names she takes from existing lists at the local art league; others she compiles from interested parents who call for more information following the appearance of a small newspaper article about the new camp that resulted from a press release Mary sent to the local news outlets. (More about PR for your camp will be covered in Chapter 6.)

Mary happily notes the newspaper article has generated a lot of interest from parents of six- to eight-year-olds. However, she's interested to see that it also generated many questions about whether the camp would consider serving nine- and ten-year-olds this year. Mary decides extending the age ranges might create a good future market for next summer. A review of the work she's done so far, however, suggests that her current market is not sufficient for including six- to eight-year-olds in her first year.

So far, so good . . .

Group size

Factors such as your camper-to-staff ratio and group size are also important considerations in planning a successful camp. As a first step in determining optimal group size, ask, "What group size is the best for the age we've targeted?"

While Figure 2.1 in the chart below does not reflect any specific group size or staffing requirement, it does provide a general guideline for group size. Your goal here should be to size your groupings so that groups run efficiently and cost-effectively, deliver maximum support of your outcomes, and are adequately supervised. The American Camping Association (ACA) standards suggest that best practice for camper supervision ratios are:

Camper Supervision Ratio

Figure 2.1

Camper Age	Staff	Group Size
4–5 years	1	6
6–8 years	1	8
9–14 years	1	10
15–18 years	1	12

Note: Your organization or state regulations may require a higher ratio.
Remember: For some activities, such as aquatics, overnights, etc., it is advisable that at least two staff members work together with a group if "team staffing" will help you better accomplish your outcomes.

Determining camp size and session length

Another question you'll need to answer is, "How big do we want our camp to be?" There will be a number of factors that contribute to the formula for your camp size.

Let's take a look. Figure 2.2 presents a useful exercise to help you assess the number of campers you want to serve.

1. **How will the number of activities affect the overall number of campers you propose to serve at one time?** The first line of the exercise below is a sample. Now try developing several different formulas by filling in the blanks.

Camp Comparison Chart

# of activity periods each day	# of campers in each activity	# of activities offered	Total number of campers
Sample:			
4 periods	10 campers	10 activities	= 400 campers
6 periods	8 campers	___ activities	= 240 campers
5 periods	24 campers	2 activities	= ___ campers
	12 campers	3 activities	= 180 campers
2 morning periods	___ campers	12 activities	= ___ campers
4 afternoon periods	___ campers	6 activites	= ___ campers
			= 60 campers

Figure 2.2

Note that your activities could be the same or different each day. Also, your number of campers may be made up of groups or individuals, that is 24 campers or 4 groups of 6 campers participate in swimming and team sports together.

2. **How does the size of the property and location of activities affect the number of campers?** Think about how much space each activity takes and how long it takes to get from one activity to the next. What is the total number of campers the site will be able to accommodate, and when and why would you need to consider opening a second site? Consider the environmental impact, especially for large groups.

3. **Determine how the number of campers you serve will affect your safety plans, marketing efforts, and staff training.** This may only have a minor effect on the number; however, your plans for these areas will have to reflect the number of campers you serve. Note that an increased numbers of campers will likely add to your staff costs.

4. **Look at determining your camper fee.** Remember, there are base-line expenses you'll incur regardless of the number of campers you have (fixed costs). With fixed costs, the fewer campers you have the higher your costs per camper will be, i.e. for pool operation. Other expenses (variable costs) increase or vary in proportion to the number of campers, i.e. costs for food and craft supplies.

5. **Consider staffing factors that affect the number of campers you have.** These include:
   • Your desired staff/camper ratio. You may need to increase the staff or cut the number of campers to maintain the ratio you want.
   • The number of activities that require a specialist or individuals with certifications to teach activities (as opposed to those any counselor can teach).

6. **Examine how children will be transported to and from camp, parking space, and distance traveling.**

Determining camp size and session length is like putting together a giant puzzle. You cannot consider any one factor—budget-related or otherwise—in isolation . . . Let's take swimming for instance. Will you offer swimming each day? If you are offering lessons, you will have fewer swimmers at the pool than if it is free swim. However, for those taking lessons, classes probably will need to return each day to continue working on their skills.

If swimmers are trying to complete a Red Cross swimming level, they may need more swimming periods than once each day for a week. If you are sharing the pool with other groups or the general public, you will need to make arrangements for use and know who is responsible for guarding or teaching classes. This will affect the number of staff, specialized training, and the ratio you need at the activity.

How large the pool is, the depth, and whether most of your campers are non-swimmers (and will be in the shallow water) will affect the numbers you can have at each period. Your fee and the overall numbers driving your budgeting change due to these factors. This is true whether you own the pool, or are paying for pool operation. How far the pool is from other activity areas and how much time it will take for children to change their clothes before and after swimming also will affect both the numbers and length of the period.

Don't worry if you don't have all the answers right now. You may not be able to decide on the number of campers you want at your day camp until you have worked through the program design and budget chapters.

Length of session

In addition to identifying the age of your campers and appropriate group size, you'll need to determine length of your session. Generally, a session reflects the time your campers will need to accomplish your program's stated outcomes. A session consists of a number of hours within a given timeframe (for example, a "program day"). A session can be defined in a number of ways; for example, if your research indicates an optimal camp plan calls for thirty hours of program time, you might consider a session that is:

- 7 hours a day for 5 days
- 7 hours a day for 4 weeks
- 8 hours a day for 4 days plus an overnight
- 6 hours for 1 day a week for 5 weeks, with a new group coming each day of the week.

Whatever session length you determine is best for your camp, you'll need to decide what hours per day—and what days each week—the camp will operate. Most camps offer programs from Monday through Friday. Typical day camp sessions may range in length from five days to four weeks. Many camps allow children to attend more than one session.

In cases where your camp provides transportation, make transportation time part of your program day. Consider planing activities during transportation, especially if the trip is more than an hour. Chapter 7 will have more information on transportation; for now, though, consider transportation as a major factor in your session design.

As you determine the length of your session, consider:

- the ability of your prospective campers to pay for their time at camp, or your ability to provide resources for camperships;
- whether you plan to have volunteer or paid staff (see Chapter 4 for more on staffing);
- your program opportunities, and the depth and breadth of skills you hope to teach;
- site availability;
- competition with other programs and services in the community; and
- the needs of the families in your target population.

Forging your vision: program opportunities.

Put simply, your program opportunities are those elements of your camp that get you down the road toward accomplishing your outcomes. Opportunities can range from simple acquisition of a specific skill, to the successful accomplishment of a broader developmental outcome for your campers.

For this reason, like all other aspects of your camp's operation, *your program opportunities must solidly support your identified outcomes.* Your program opportunities will play a key role, not only in the day-to-day success of your camp operation, but in helping shape the camp culture, or community, that will be a critical component in the overall success of your camp.

Take a moment to again review your mission statement and list of outcomes. Now, list and rank your outcomes, adding the corresponding program opportunities; for example, activities that will help you deliver outcomes to your campers. Ask yourself how the successful completion of an archery or swimming program will support an outcome committed to building confidence. Finally, in what way will the overall culture of your camp support and complement this opportunity, and, by doing so, reinforce your outcomes? (See the CD-ROM for a chart to rank your outcomes.)

Taking a systematic look at how the specifics of your program support your outcomes is a great way of determining your program focus. Doing this regularly also is a good way to ensure your program remains "spot on" with your outcomes.

The issue to bear in mind here is the same thought you'll need to carry with you every step of the way through your planning process and beyond: everything you do—administratively and program-related—*must support your outcomes.*

Assessing the competition

No matter how great the vision or mission of your camp, if it brings nothing new to your community, or if another camp in your area is already doing what you propose to do, chances are good that it will be hard to successfully establish and maintain your camp.

Unless you know that the competing camp has a large waiting list and does not plan to expand, it will be difficult, if not impossible, to market your camp against your competition. Day camps, like any other industry, can be competitive. This competition can be a significantly limiting factor for the new camp that is going up against an established camp already serving the needs of the community.

Because of this, it is important to carry out an evaluation of the other camps in your area, especially those that may have a mission and goals similar to yours. It is equally important that you compare these camps and (how they benefit the camper) with your camp's mission and benefits.

"Being aware of what is out there and how you can develop your niche is essential," says DD Gass, Assistant Executive Director for Camp Fire USA Day Camps in Des Moines, Iowa. "Find out what your program can bring to community that others aren't, and how you can be unique. One way to do this is networking with your community. We do a lot of that."

The best place to begin is simply by asking around your community. Find out what camps are in operation. Order and review marketing material of other camps. Or, if you can, visit competing camps and ask questions, or visit camps similar to the one you are planning in another community. Do your homework. As you carry out your investigation, try to get a feel for how well the camp is meeting the needs of the community. Would people who've had experience with the camp recommend it to their friends? Why? Why not? How successful are competing camps in fulfilling their stated goals, mission, and outcomes in the eyes of the community and their campers? How long have they been in business?

The next step involves taking a close look at your camp in comparison to existing programs. What will your camp deliver that the existing camps do not? How do these deliverables match up to the community needs you've identified earlier in this chapter? And don't forget the most important question: How effectively will your camp support outcomes the community needs compared to your competition?

You can document this activity by charting the information in a matrix similar to that shown in Figure 2.3.

After you've completed this exercise, you should be able to identify the single most significant competitive advantage your camp will have over the competition. Once you know that, you'll be on your way to developing the kind of camp your community and campers will value and support.

This information also will help identify a key marketing advantage. Once you determine how your camp differs, file it away; we'll be coming back to it in our discussion of marketing for your camp in Chapter 6.

Paying the piper: funding and scholarships

Money isn't everything, but it's an important consideration when you're planning an effective day camp program. As often as not, good funding equates with a strong and effective camp program. If nothing else, good funding can bring many options—activity-related and otherwise—to your program. That's why early in your

Existing Programs

Figure 2.3

Camps in the area	Camp	Camp	Camp	Camp	Camp
Type of camp					
Target population					
How long in business					
Program focus					
Session length					
Services (i.e. trans- portation, food, etc.)					
# of campers per day					
Fee					

planning process you'll need to take a good hard look at how your program will be funded. You will need to separate start-up costs from yearly on-going expenses.

In some cases, foundations or corporations are willing to fund start-up costs for not-for-profits. For-profits may need to secure investors for these expenses. Most on-going costs are handled through camper fees, organization subsidy, or scholarships. More information on budgeting will be found in Chapter 4.

Scholarships

Scholarships—or as they're called in the camp community "camperships"—are an important part of some day camp funding plans. Camperships enable those with limited means to enjoy the considerable benefits of a camp experience. For the individual child, a campership can mean the difference between benefiting from a day camp experience or not. For the camp, camperships can be an excellent way to build good community relations, help the under-served and ensure a good mix and diversity for a camp.

There are a variety of ways to fund camperships. Some camps actually budget an amount specifically for providing this service to needy children. Many not-for-profit camps undertake campaigns or participate in community drives with other camps to fund camperships. Donations to not-for-profits are tax-exempt.

Good proposals, brochures, and other informational outreach can do much to encourage people to give money for the worthy purpose of sending a child to camp. Some organizations hold sales to fund camperships. Young people also can sometimes earn their way to camp by selling a product that supports the organization and provides a campership incentive for the child.

The number of camperships will depend somewhat on your target population. If your camp is serving children from low-income populations, or children with disabilities, you may need a larger pool of campership dollars. If your regular program and your campership program will be serving children from highly varied cultural or socio-economic backgrounds you may need to consider the impact on the feelings of those involved. Will children be challenged to fit in; might group interactions be unusually difficult; will peer attitudes or preconceptions be a problem?

Most camps have a campership request form a parent can submit for a full or partial campership. The application includes a description of the process, guidelines, and deadlines. Some campers qualify if their family is on welfare or other government subsidy.

Others may have special family situations or emergencies that qualify them for camperships, such as a fire in their home, high medical bills, or a death in the family. Consider establishing a committee to select individuals who will receive this type of assistance.

It is important that every child—whether he or she is attending camp on a campership or not—is treated equally. At times you, the camp director, may need to step forward to make sure the camper has the proper clothes and shoes, and a day-pack like others to pack their clothes in. You may also need to ensure that they have lunch and transportation to and from camp. Some camps maintain stockpiles of donated clothes, swimsuits, towels and shoes for children that do not have these things or have lost theirs.

Courtesy of Merri-Mac for Girls, Black Mountain, North Carolina

Meanwhile, back at Camp ARTastic . . .

Mary schedules a special meeting with the board to discuss the possibility of adding six new camperships for "gifted kids in need." For her first season, all start-up funding is covered by her sponsoring organization, the Culver City Art League. However, as she plans her program, she remains mindful of the possible opportunity to expand funding sources in the years ahead; she researches grants that are available for programs such as hers, and begins looking for fits between her program and specific grant requirements. The board grants her three camperships; this, in turn, will well-position Mary to fulfill the requirements of a grant she plans to seek next year.

Partnering with parents

The experienced day camp administrator knows that there is no more important ally in ensuring a successful camp program than the parents of a camp's participants. Educators have long been aware of the essential supportive role engaged parents play in a child's academic career. The same is true for camp. In addition to serving as a valuable volunteer or paid staff resource for a camp (where appropriate), parents can supplement the value a camp brings to a child. This can occur in even simple, non-direct ways; for instance, by reviewing with a child the things he or she has learned during the camp day and thereby reinforcing lessons that support camp outcomes.

Because of this, the wants and needs of the parents in your target population are among the most important considerations you will have as a day camp administrator. One of your first and most important duties will be to help the parents of your prospective campers make decisions about whether your camp is right for their children.

Outreach to parents is critical, both to the on-going success of your camp and its effective marketing. As any camp director will tell you, no brochure, Web site or advertisement equals good word-of mouth endorsement from parents who have experience with a camp. (And, by extension, nothing has the potential to damage a camp's reputation as a dissatisfied parent.)

Good outreach to parents of prospective campers begins with thorough, accurate, and well-written information about your camp in your marketing campaign and other materials. Remember, your marketing materials reflect on your camp; they must be professional, informative, and engaging. In addition to presenting your overall mission and program scope, these materials should inform parents about philosophic and operational specifics; for example, whether your camp requires additional fees for special activities, how you handle children with special needs, or even something as basic as lunch arrangements.

It is important that your materials are focused clearly to address specific informational needs. Don't try to cram everything into your brochure. Instead, break up the information parents need to know. For instance, consider discussing general camp philosophy and mission in your brochure, and placing other information parents need to know (what kids need to bring to camp, for example) in a follow-up letter. This will free your brochure to do what it does best: tell your camp story free of the clutter of incidental information.

Some parents may have little experience with camps. They may also not understand the benefits camping brings to children. For this reason, as camp director you'll be educating parents as well as their children. For parents new to the camp experience, a recommendation from you to visit the parents' section of the American Camping Association Web site (www.acadcamps.org/parents/) can be a great first step in recruiting a new ardent convert to the camping fold, *and* creating a loyal ally of your camp.

When it comes to parent questions about your program, they often fall into three key areas:

- *"What do I need to know to make the decision to send my child to your camp?"* This type of question can be addressed through your brochure, Web site, video, or via telephone contact.
- *"What do I need to do to prepare my child for camp?"* This type of question can be addressed through a follow-up letter, Web site, video, or via telephone contact.
- *"What do I need to know each day (or week) while my child is in camp?"* This type of question can be addressed through daily "backpack notes," via telephone, or Web site.)

Partnerships with parents are essential. According to Jeff Ackerman, director of Elmwood Country Day Camp, maintaining a strong focus on cultivating and maintaining good and active relationships with parents is key to his camp's success. Elmwood, a private day camp in Westchester, New York, serves about 450 young people a season.

"Partnering with parents is vital," says Ackerman. "It's critical that the parent recognizes that you are working with them to help the child grow, develop and learn rather than just provide a safe recreational experience. Parents play an integral role in the success of our camp."

Because day camp provides an opportunity to work in partnership with parents on a daily basis, it goes without saying that it is important to establish an on-going, positive relationship with them. To do this:

- Never miss an opportunity to communicate with a parent about your program, his or her child's development, or any special needs.
- Be prepared to answer questions. You'll get a lot of them. While you might delegate one person to address parents' questions, it is imperative that you and each and every member of your staff be prepared to provide adequate and satisfactory responses to any and all parent inquiries that might come up.
- Consider setting up a parents advisory committee to review and provide on-going feedback and input on your program.

Your day camp community should extend far beyond your campers and staff. For it to be the rich and supportive complement to your program it can be, a camp community should be an extended family, one that includes community members (for instance in advisory roles) and, most important, parents. Planning your camp to foster this sense of extended family will be important in ensuring maximum buy-in and support from your community and benefits for your campers.

[Notes]

1. Armand & Beverly Ball, 2000. *Basic Camp Management:* American Camping Association. p. 18

Courtesy of Camp Tall Turf, Grand Rapids, Michigan/Denise Fase

Chapter 3

The Cornerstone—Beginning to Design Your Program

As you begin to put together a successful day camp program, it is useful to establish what a program *is not*. For instance, it is not a random collection of activities you select simply because you see a good staffing fit, or you think your campers will like swimming. Your program includes everything you do in camp from the time campers arrive until they leave. Actually, if your camp arranges transportation, your program also includes what happens from the time campers are picked up until they are dropped off at the end of the day.

Putting together what will be the centerpiece of your camp—your program—is anything but an exercise in grab-bag program development. A strong and effective day camp program must begin with a focused and strategic approach, and clearly link outcomes and program elements.

True, your program must offer activities that your campers will enjoy and are possible to accomplish in your camp's setting. And your activities must be in line with your staffing and budget resources. But, most important, each and every activity you include in your overall camp program *must solidly support your outcomes*. After all, changing lives through programs based on well-supported outcomes is really the highest mission of any day camp program.

But *how* do you put together a program that supports a specific set of outcomes? For instance, what is the relationship, if any, between archery or weaving (and how your staff teaches them) and the stated outcome of "increased ability to work cooperatively with others"? How can you be sure that your activities and other program attributes are suited to drive measurable developmental improvement in your campers? And how do

"The best thing we like hearing from our campers is that they can't wait to come back the next day. I know our program has done a good job when I hear campers say 'I can't wait to come back tomorrow' or 'I can't wait to come back next year.' That's when I know we've done things right."

—Chris Winkler, YMCA Camp Eagle Rock, Charlotte, North Carolina

you assemble the many and varied elements of your program to ensure that your camp day delivers a cohesive, workable, balanced program, one that your campers will enjoy *and* that supports your outcomes?

Is putting together a program that covers all these bases easy? Well, let's just say that formulating a good program is not as effortless as beginning each camp day by looking at the sky and saying, "Hmmm . . . Look's like a good day for horseshoes!"

But, take heart. While good program development may well be one of the biggest challenges you'll face as a new day camp director, the biggest challenges, as the saying goes, are usually the best *opportunities*. From now on, think of the program you'll be developing as the best opportunity you'll have to make your camp everything you want it to be.

Developing you camp's program to support your outcomes

You already know that identifying and supporting your outcomes should be your single most important criteria guiding the selection of activities. Common sense, of course, plays a part in the activity selection process. For instance, your activities should be age-appropriate, and provide enough variety to keep your campers engaged, interested, and "on the move" developmentally.

The following is a six-step process to help you map your way through program development.

- **Step one: Mission** — Determine the purpose or reason for our existence.
- **Step two: Outcomes** — Identify the youth development benefits or changes desired.
- **Step three: Activities** — Undertake the actions to best achieve these outcomes.

- **Step four: Inputs** — Allocate the resources needed to do this.
- **Step five: Outputs** — Ascertain the numbers we plan to serve or the number of activities or times offered.
- **Step six: Indicators** — Verify that participants have changed because evidence of progress can be identified.

You have already determined your mission and outcomes. Let's start with exploring step three.

Begin by listing all the activities or actions you can think of to best achieve these outcomes. Remember to include all actions that affect your outcomes, including how you organize you camper groups, start and end the day, and how campers are assigned or choose activities.

Now determine the resources (or inputs) your campers and staff will need in order to participate in the activity or accomplish the action. List all the equipment and supplies, number of staff and training needed, and other resources.

Remember, outputs are primarily numbers—the number of activities, the number of groups, the number that participated in an activity, and so on. Outputs also include your budget projections or total number of campers. The board or owner may want to know your outputs and whether you have indicators that show you've achieved your outcomes.

Keep in mind that just because your campers attended your program does not automatically mean they will come out of the camp experience reflecting a change. Outcomes are realized only when you have measurable indicators showing there indeed has been a change in a camper's behavior. Successful achievement of an outcome means that staff, campers and/or parents can observe indicators or see a difference between the time campers start camp and during or after camp is finished.

Figure 3.1 is an example of the process for monitoring an outcome. The chart will help your staff identify the outcome, know what your activities should achieve, and be aware of what kind of change to look for. Use of a chart such as this will give your staff a better idea of whether they are being successful with their campers. This example and a blank chart are on your CD.

As you progress in your planning, this diagram can serve as a valuable touchstone you'll want to revisit. For now, let's try a quick exercise to help you begin selecting the activities that will be the backbone of you camp program.

First, let's review the top twenty most popular activities of ACA-accredited day camps. These are specific activities; the list does not include all the other actions that help you achieve your outcomes. ACA asks day camps to rate the top ten activities they would most like to offer to potential campers and their parents. The activity ranking is based on a calculation. Figure 3.2 is a ranking of the top twenty most popular day camp activities.

Monitoring Outcomes

Figure 3.1

Outcomes	Activities	Inputs	Outputs	Indicators
Sample: Increased ability to work with others	All	Staff trained in positive group development, conflict resolution	Ratio of 1 staff to 6 to 8 campers (depending on age) 4 groups of same age per unit 5 units	Shows progress in cooperation during week Demonstrates ability to share and takes turns on at least 3 occasions More compromise and less group conflict by end of week
	Team sports	Equipment Field Staff knowledgeable of game rules	Play 3 different games during the week	
	Clean up Skits Cookout	Group area designated Recognition for clean area Clean up equipment	Clean group area once a day	
		Costumes and props	Each group performs a skit	
		Food Staff trained in safely organizing cookouts Cookout area Equipment	One cookout per week	

Most Popular Day Camp Activities

Figure 3.2

(Ranked in order of popularity)

Activity	Rank
Arts/crafts	1
Swimming—recreational	2
Nature/environmental studies	3
Counselor-in-training program	4
Basketball	5
Sports—field and team	6
Camping skills/outdoor living	7
Field trips	8
Drama	9
Soccer	10
Archery	11
Aquatic activities	12
Hiking	13
Leadership development	14
Swimming—instructional	15
Team-building activities	16
Baseball/softball	17
Canoeing	18
Challenge/rope courses	19
Music	20

Now, it's your turn. With your outcomes from Chapter 1 clearly in mind, begin thinking about your activities, and how you'd rank them. Remember, your list can include activities not on the above list. Try compiling your list on the template titled "Most Popular Day Camp Activities" included on your CD.

Your selection and ranking should clearly reflect support for your outcomes. Remember the old real estate motto: "Location, location, location." When it comes to day camp administration, you could well put it this way: "Outcomes, outcomes, outcomes."

Now, let's compare your list to the responses given by other day camps. Don't forget, these camps have *hundreds* of years of collective experience in program development; looking at how they function can be very instructive.

To begin, go to ACA's Web site at www.ACAcamps.org. Locate the "Find a camp" section and select a camp-type that is most similar to the one you are planning. Click on "Interest Areas" and select "Day Camp."

Now, choose a day camp with the same length of session, affiliation, gender served (coed, all boy, or all girl,) and, if possible, the same region of the country. Compare the top-ten activities at the three camps you have selected. How do these compare with the activities you're considering? As you do your homework, pay particular attention to whether, in your view, these camps' activities achieve the outcomes listed on ACA's Web page.

The next task is an excellent place to begin evaluating specific activities—and how they support your outcomes—to the next level.

As you evaluate a potential activity, always begin by asking, "Will this support my outcomes?" (Hopefully, you're not tired of asking that question. You'll be asking it a lot more between now and your first day of camp!)

If your answer is "Yes, this activity *does* support my outcomes," ask, "How?" As long as you're doing the exercise, you may as well grab a pen and paper to capture your answers; you'll want to come back to this information later as you select and refine the final contents of your program. The worksheet you create for this exercise might look something like this:

"Will this activity support my outcomes?"

- If **yes** — How? _____
_____

- If **no** — Is there *any* link I can draw between this activity and any of my outcomes? If not, is there any way this link can be established by developing any innovative or unique way to present and teach this activity? If so, can I list it here? _____
_____
_____

Staying creative in your planning

Sometimes linking an activity with an outcome is simply a process of developing a creative rationale, one that links outcomes and activities in new and unique ways. As you design your program, think outside the box. After all, taking a novel approach to selecting your activities can be one of the most satisfying parts of building a new program, or redesigning an existing one. Once you begin putting the activities you're evaluating through your "creative filter," you'll be surprised at how many new ways you can think of to support your outcomes. A great way to expand the scope and content of your program is to uncover unlikely activity-outcome links, and spin them into new and innovative ways of supporting your outcomes.

Avoid falling into the trap of thinking that only certain activity types support particular kinds of outcomes; for instance, that a team sport like softball is necessary if you wish to improve the teamwork abilities of your campers. That's not always the case. True, some activities are a natural fit for specific outcomes: softball for building teamwork, let's say. But the real challenge resides in figuring out ways to support outcomes in new and creative ways.

Remember, activities can support outcomes in ways that are not always obvious. Often, *how* an activity is presented and taught *plays as much, or more significant, a role* than the activity itself in supporting a given outcome. For this reason, you must bring imagination and creativity to the tasks of choosing, teaching, and even scheduling activities.

For example, let's take an arts and crafts program that has a desired outcome of increasing creativity. For this program, the staff might assemble the supplies in kits with patterns, or simply offer kits that contain a variety of supplies. While patterns may be easier for both campers and staff, they may not be as creative. Yet, the stated outcome is "increasing small motor skills," and a detailed kit may be better than just a kit full of supplies.

Your teaching approach can also support outcomes. If the outcome is based on fostering creativity, the staff should encourage original thinking during the activity, not just ask kids to follow a pattern. To help increase small motor skills, you can demonstrate progress by selecting projects that are increasingly more difficult.

Your teaching approach and activity set-up should support your desired outcome. A camp might have both of these outcomes; it might decide to have kits that can be decorated in a creative manner, or supplies with which children can practice different techniques, improving their creativity and small motor skills. A finished product completed by a talented staff as an example may actually discourage creativity; however, it may help a camper measure their ability to complete something correctly (small motor skills).

The important point here is your program design should not end with deciding on the activity. Once your camp is in full swing, as part of your on-going training you'll need to continually emphasize to your staff the importance of knowing the desired outcome and helping children achieve it. This will enable your camp to offer a diverse, exciting, and outcome-focused experience.

Let's check in at Camp ARTastic and see how Mary is making out as she works through her program planning.

Activities and scheduling at Camp ARTastic

Mary sits at her crowded desk, her head in her hand, asking herself, "How did I get into this?" (If she would have just reviewed the recommendations in this chapter, she might be saying instead, "This isn't as hard as I thought! This is going to be a great program. And a lot of fun!")

With her outcomes clearly in mind, Mary begins sorting through the many art activities she's considering for her program. The outcomes are as follows:

- gain ability in using different art media for creative expression,
- increase enjoyment and understanding of basic art concepts, and
- show improved willingness to share with others and use materials safely and respectfully.

Her camp committee has given her some direction—she knows, for instance, that the camp will offer elementary drawing and ceramics classes, but she hasn't decided if they will select a third or other activity they might do as a group.

Want to join Mary in another challenge? Think of an activity that's traditionally identified with building good teamwork (let's use softball as our example again) and try to come up a way to link it with an outcome with which it's usually not identified. Ask: "As a result of this activity, my day campers will build and strengthen key emotional competencies." Get creative: do you see a link between softball and emotional competencies?

You may. Or you may find it too much of a stretch. Either way, the point is that during the process of shifting through and selecting activities that may not, at first glance, appear to support your outcomes, you can, with a little research and creativity, find a new relevance for an unlikely activity. With a little digging, you may very well find there is indeed a link between softball and emotional development.

Maybe you or your organization have already identified the perfect activities for your program. Maybe you've already shifted, sorted, and selected your activities. Good. But remember, a program is not just about how the activities are taught. Other factors such as how these activities are scheduled will also play an important role in your program's overall look and feel.

Planning the daily schedule

You've figured out what activities you'll be offering. The next step is to organize them into a daily schedule. To do this, however, it's useful to look at the role a good program structure plays in an effective program.

Your structure is almost as important as your activities. For example, if your outcomes are based on improving group-based social skills, you will probably want to plan your camp days in such a way that the group experience is enhanced by doing activities together.

If outcomes call for more individual skill-building, consider designing your activities in ways that address the needs, promote the interests, and build the skills of the individual camper. The group staying together will be less important than the individual progress of each camper. Each camper may have their own activity schedule or classes. For example, if you've decided that decision making is an important outcome for an individual or group, you may want to give your campers more opportunities to choose the activities they want to participate in individually or as a group. If conflict resolution skills are an important outcome, they need opportunities to make decisions and interact as a group.

Now let's start making up your daily schedule. A daily schedule gives needed structure and balance to the camp day. Consider the following as you begin to develop your schedule:

- the number and length of activity periods,
- a balance between high- and low-energy activities,
- age appropriateness,
- all-camp and small group activities, and
- lunch and quiet time.

Meanwhile, back at Camp ARTastic, Mary reviews her outcomes. With these in mind, Mary projects she'll be able to offer three core classes. All of her projected thirty students, she envisions, will rotate through these classes each day. Each class will have ten students and be offered three times a day. Even the rotation and numbers in each class support Mary's outcomes.

In addition to the classes, she plans an art show at the end of each week for their parents. Campers will spend one period each day planning the show. Campers can sign up for what they want to do to help put the show together. Some of the options will be to prepare and serve a snack, make decorations, set up the exhibit, make invitations, and clean up. At the same time, she begins to makes notes of the resources (inputs) she need to put her staffing plan and budget together.

The sample schedule in Figure 3.3 is an example of the daily schedule Mary put together. Use the blank schedule on your CD to plan your schedule.

Camp Wellspring Daily Schedule

Figure 3.3

Time	Activity
8:00 to 8:15	Opening
8:30 to 8:45	Small group meeting
9:00 to 10:15	Activity period #1
10:30 to 11:45	Activity period #2
12:00 to 12:45	Lunch
1:00 to 1:45	Quiet activity period
2:00 to 3:15	Activity period #3
3:30 to 3:45	Small group time
3:45 to 4:00	Closing

As you complete your daily schedule, you'll need to decide if every day will follow the same schedule. For example, will your camp observe a different schedule for the first and last day, special all-camp events, overnights, and so on?

Although the daily routine will vary from camp to camp, some cornerstones of the camp day are common to the schedules of most operations.

- **Arrival and opening ceremony** — This may include ways for all campers to gather in a central location at the beginning of the day. It might include a flag ceremony, announcements, and meeting with their counselor in small groups.
- **Small group meeting** — This is the time the counselor gets together with their camper group to get organized and discuss the plans for the day.
- **Morning and afternoon activity periods** — This is the time when campers participate in the specific activities available. There may be one or two periods each morning or afternoon. This decision will depend on how much you want to accomplish, number of activities offered, and the time it takes to travel between those activities.
- **Lunch** — Lunch at camps can range from hot meals for the whole group to sack lunches that are eaten while campers are in their small groups. There may also be special times the entire camp has a picnic or when the small group has a cookout.

- **Rest hour or quiet time** — These often happen after lunch or at times when the children need to slow down and do quiet activities due to heat, or just to rest.
- **All-camp activities** — This includes theme-centered activities for the whole camp. These activities may be daily morning or afternoon themes, or a special day that happens once or twice a week.
- **Closing ceremony** — This is usually the gathering at the end of the day. Small groups may reflect on the day and talk about the plans for the next day. There also may be a flag lowering or other closing activity for the entire camp before dividing up for transportation home.
- **Pre- and post-camp activities** — If the camp provides activities to meet the child-care needs of some families, arrange groups by length of day or schedule special activities for those who will arrive early and/or stay late.

Creating camp themes and events

Many camps plan their programs using a theme for the entire camp season, a new theme for each session, or a special day. These themes can include, for example: Cultural Awareness Week, Pioneer Week, Wonder Olympics, Zoo Camp, and Circus Day. Groups might prepare for the day by making decorations, bringing or making costumes, and coming up with an activity or skit to share with other groups.

The activities also could be designed by staff and presented for groups to rotate from activity to activity as a group. If there is a central gathering place for the event, individual campers may rotate to activities on their own. These decisions will once again be dependent on your outcomes.

For example, if the theme is Camp Carnival there might be balloons and colored signs promoting each station. Campers and staff may dress like clowns or other carnival characters. Stations could be either run by staff or individuals rotated from each camper group. Remember, you'll need enough stations for most of the campers to be active and not waiting in long lines. Points can be accumulated for the group or an individual winner. In making the event-related decision always ask *what will best help campers achieve the outcome.*

If you plan the program in such a way that individuals participate without their group, consider encouraging them to stay with a buddy.

Individual stations might be:

- **Soak the clown** — A staff or camper stands with their head through a poncho hung on a line. Campers get three sponges and a point for each time they hit the clown.

- **Lights out** — Place three lit candles on a platform or bench. Campers are given a squirt gun and have three shots to put a candle out. If they do, they get a point.
- **Giant horseshoes** — Place three pegs in the ground about two feet apart. The camper is given three hula-hoops; he or she gets a point for each peg he or she rings (without including another peg or leaning on a peg).

If the program is designed for groups, the group must stay together as they go from station to station. Activities could be timed with a horn or whistle, or a number for the order of station progression given to each group. Group relays might be:

- **Soak the clown** — Two teams line up and each camper takes a turn at throwing a sponge at their counselor who has their head in a poncho as above. The team making the most hits wins a point.
- **Walk the tightrope** — Two 2 x 4 x 10 boards are placed parallel on the ground about eight feet apart. Each team lines up at the end of the board and each camper must walk the tightrope. The first team to get all their campers across the tightrope wins a point. (Teams must be the same size or some members go more than once.)
- **Dive for the pearl** — Each team has a large pail with white beads and sand in the bottom and a plastic cup. Teams line up and each camper runs to the pail and "dives" for one pearl. When they find a pearl, they place it in the plastic cup and anther team member runs forward to dive. The first team with all their members finding a pearl wins a point. (Teams must be the same size.)

Other stations could offer snacks (cotton candy or popcorn) or face painting. Campers could use the points they earn to "pay" at these stations.

Other ideas for themes include:

- Crazy Olympic Day
- Backwards Day (start in PJs, or wear clothes backwards)
- Superhero
- Beach Day, Fun in the Sun
- Circus Day
- International Festival
- On with the Show
- Hawaiian Luau
- Winter Wonderland (or Christmas in July)
- Wild Wild West
- Cartoon Day or Disney Day

- Jungle Adventure (with the zoo or nature center bringing animals to camp, obstacle courses, compass hikes)
- Pirate Day (with hidden treasures)
- Wacky Wear Day (with wild hairdos, crazy outfits, dress up your counselor, make crazy hats)
- Nature themes like Geology Rocks, Nature Shutterbugs, or Mammal Madness
- Popular movie themes such as *Star Wars* or Harry Potter's Hogwart's School of Witchcraft, *Wizard of OZ*, *Finding Nemo*
- TV themes such as *CSI* — mystery investigation, *Survivor*, or *The Amazing Race*
- Hunt themes such as treasure hunts, dinosaur egg hunt (watermelon), counselor hunts, scavenger hunts, etc.

The list, which can go on and on, is limited only by your imagination. The important thing is to keep events exciting and moving. But don't lose control. Staff needs to understand the plan and their role. Some camps let the campers choose a theme; some prefer not to announce the theme until campers are at camp so some sessions don't become more or less popular than others.

Creating group or individual activity schedules

Before you design the master schedule, you must decide whether campers will remain in the same group all or most of the day, or whether they will take part in activities as an individual. You also need to decide who makes the decision about the activities they participate in—the camper(s) or the administration (or counselor). An individual schedule is made if the camper participates in activities without being part of any one group. Group schedules outline the camp day for a camp group. This gives you four basic approaches to activity scheduling. Number one is where the *camper group* chooses and signs up for activities after they arrive, which permits greater group choice. Number two is where the *individual campers* choose the activities they want and then sign up for the activity. Number three is where the *group participates* in a schedule fully planned by the administration. Number four is where individuals are *given a schedule* to follow. Some camps do a combination for different times of the day or days of the week.

In a matrix, the four choices might look like Figure 3.4.

If decision making or youth empowerment is one of your outcomes, you may wish to pursue a less-structured scheduling. Set the basic opening and closing time;

Group Schedule Matrix

Figure 3.4

1	2
Group participates together Group chooses activities	Individuals participate alone Individual chooses activities
3	4
Group participates together Administration assigns activities	Individuals participate alone Administration assigns activities

you can schedule it based on the arrangements for lunch. Campers then make the decisions about what they want to do, and when.

The advantage of less structure is the choice it brings to your campers to make decisions as a group, work on cooperation, and shape their camp day. In these settings where there is less structure, campers and their counselors typically plan their weekly schedule, generally on the first day of camp.

For safety reasons, a schedule completed by a camper group should be shared with the administration, and added to the master schedule. In some cases, a combination of pre-determined and flexible schedules may be best suited to your program. When it is, your campers should plan for activities with their counselor; you can schedule for them (or they can sign up for) any activities that require a certified specialist, such as swimming, horseback riding, or challenge activities.

Regardless of whether you set the schedule or campers select activities when they come, you will still want to have the basic daily schedule discussed earlier in the chapter to provide a clear, well-defined framework in which to plan activities. It provides your parents with a solid routine that can greatly assist them in planning around jobs or other personal demands.

Do not underestimate the importance of scheduling to support your outcomes. If your outcomes call for a strong focus on individual skill-building, whenever possible schedule activities so children have a chance to improve their skills by doing the activity more than once.

For example, if the outcome calls for the achievement of a specific skill consider designing the program so individual campers progress individually as their skills improve. You also can give campers time to sign up for the activities they want to participate in individually as an alternative to working with their group.

Of course, to make this workable you may need to establish limits on how many participants can sign up for any activity at a given time (for instance due to limited staff or material resources.)

Whatever the scheduling perimeters you eventually set for your camp, keep one thing in mind: As in every facet of your camp, *achieving your outcomes—those things you want to cultivate and grow in your campers—should be your primary consideration.*

Use the sample Day Camp Group Schedule in Figure 3.5 to start sketching out how one of your groups might plan its day.

Day Camp Group Schedule

Counselor _____ The week of_____

	Morning	Lunch	Afternoon	Outcomes
Monday				
Tuesday				
Wednesday				
Thursday				
Friday				

Figure 3.5

Courtesy of Blue Star Camps, Hendersonville, North Carolina

Creating a master schedule

You know how you're going to schedule the camp day for your individual campers or groups. Now you'll need to bring together these various schedules into a master schedule. A master schedule coordinates individuals or groups enabling the overall camp to run efficiently, on schedule and smoothly. You'll find that it's easier to plan the master schedule for groups instead of individuals.

As the name suggests, a master schedule lets you monitor all activities, groups and individuals. It provides an at-a-glance way to know, at any point in the camp day, what is going on, who is doing it, and whether your day is on schedule.

A group master schedule for the week might look like the one in Figure 3.6.

Up for another exercise? If the group plans their own schedule, try creating six hypothetical group schedules, then folding them into a master matrix. Perhaps you've already begun planning your camp's scheduling. If so, use the exercise to develop, schedule-wise, your own master plan. (Remember, worksheets and planning matrixes such as those on the accompanying CD-ROM can be easily customized for use with your camp.)

Designing your operational plan

A program operational plan acts as an overall strategic framework for examining each of your activities in the context of your overall program. It allows you to capture in a single document ten key functions/attributes of an activity, including outcomes, physical location, staff requirements, safety rules and others.

Actually, a program operational plan is simply an exercise that enables you to bring the same strategic focus to activity planning selection that you've already used in determining your outcomes.

Figure 3.7 shows a typical plan. Note the ten functions and attributes the sheet shows for an activity. (You can use the template on your CD-ROM to develop your own plan.)

One more thing: Be sure to retain a copy of your operational plan for each activity for your staff manual.

Day Camp Master Schedule

Figure 3.6

Morning	Monday	Tuesday	Wednesday	Thursday	Friday
Activity #1					
Swimming	Group 1	Group 4	Group 3	Group 2	Groups 1 & 2
Arts/crafts	Group 2	Group 1	Group 4	Group 3	
Archery	Group 3	Group 2	Group 1	Group 4	Groups 3 & 4
Nature	Group 4	Group 3	Group 2	Group 1	Plan for Carnival
Activity #2					
Swimming	Group 2	Group 1	Group 4	Group 3	Groups 3 & 4
Arts/crafts	Group 3	Group 2	Group 1	Group 4	
Archery	Group 4	Group 3	Group 2	Group 1	Groups 1 & 2 Plan for
Nature	Group 1	Group 4	Group 3	Group 2	Carnival
Lunch and Quiet Time	w/Group	Picnic	w/Group	w/Group	Carnival Food

Afternoon

	Monday	Tuesday	Wednesday	Thursday	Friday
Activity #3					
Swimming	Group 3	Group 2	Group 1	Group 4	
Field sports	Group 4	Group 3	Group 2	Group 1	All-camp
Camp skills	Group 1	Group 4	Group 3	Group 2	Carnival
Hiking	Group 2	Group 1	Group 4	Group 3	

Program Activity Operational Plan

Figure 3.7

1. Activity

2. Outcomes

3. Location/boundaries/controlled access

4. Eligibility requirements for participants (age, height, experience, competency demonstration, etc.)

5. Staff qualifications, certification, and/or skill verification

6. Camper/staff supervision ratio

7. Equipment needed, including protective equipment

8. Equipment maintenance procedures and responsibility, access policies, etc.

9. Safety orientation (when required and by whom)

10. Safety rules

Looking at your program's budget implications

Wouldn't it be nice if you could plan the day camp program of your dreams without having to worry about a budget?

That's why you must consider the budget implications of everything you do at *every* step of the way of your planning process, and throughout your program administration. However, budget should not determine your desired youth development outcomes. The activity is the tool to achieve the outcome. You may have to change an activity or do it differently if your budget dictates.

Hopefully by now, you have a good idea of how to achieve your outcomes through well-planned program activities. You know how to select activities and schedule them to help support your outcomes. You and your staff will know the indicators that show that you've achieved your outcome. You should also have become familiar with the value of a "Program Activity Operational Plan" in helping you evaluate you activities strategically, and tie them back to your outcomes. And finally, you should have a good idea about how to achieve your outcomes and understand the budget implications of your decisions.

Developing your camp program can be hard work. But it also can be one of the most satisfying areas of the job of new camp director.

If the camp mission, purpose and outcomes you've identified in Chapter 1 are your camp's foundation, the program you've now erected is its structure, one that is now ready for the next stage of development.

Chapter 4

The Business of Camp

When I became a camp professional, my dad began to ask me, "When are you going to get a real job?" Some people have great difficulty thinking of camp as a real business, or a camp director's job as a real job. However, until you do, you will not be able to secure the skills and resources needed to develop effective, enriching programs and bring them to the kids who need them most.

As important as it is, developing a program that brings developmental advantages to your campers is not the only success your camp has to demonstrate. It also must be viable as a business operation. This is as true for the not-for-profit camp as it is for the for-profit operation.

This is not to say profit should become the all-defining focus for your camp that it is for most businesses. Instead, it means that whenever possible you should leverage proven business best practices to ensure the strength of your camp's operation over the long term. By doing this, you perform one of the most important tasks to ensure the long-term viability of your camp, and see to it that your program will continue to fulfill its mission for a long time to come.

Your business plan: your map to business viability

A good first step in any journey is looking at the map that shows the way to your destination. Your business plan is the map that charts your course to sound and proven business practices. If your camp has been around for awhile, your business plan may already be in your back pocket. If not, or if you're just starting your camp, you'll need to develop a business plan.

Courtesy of Tom Sawyer Camps, Pasadena, California

This book places a strong emphasis on planning. As you'll see, in the chapters ahead we will discuss plans of many types, among them program plans, operational plans, staff plans, market plans, strategic plans, business plans, and risk management plans. Let's begin by looking at the elements of a plan that will be key to your organization's success: your business plan.

Some believe that a business plan is warranted only when there's a need to support a new product or service, or the expansion of a current organization. The truth is that a business plan can deliver value at every step of your camp's operation. A sample business plan outline, in Figure 4.1 (and on the CD-ROM), provides the basic structure of an effective plan.

This outline gives you a working structure for a new business. It integrates information from plans covered elsewhere in this book, including the strategic plan (purpose, outcomes, audience, direction, and goals), the market plan (market, unique position, communications, promotion) and the operational/management plan (program, staff, risk management, administration). The outline also provides some detail on the short- and long-range financial plan (start-up costs, resources, budget, financial management systems).

If you are simply adding a new program to your camp operation, your business plan may need to only examine that program and how it affects the total operation. For example, let's say your camp has had a successful program for several years, but now you'd like to add a field trip on one day. Ask how will this affect your income and expenses, market, risks, and so on. And, of course, ask: "Will it help achieve my outcomes?"

You can create a business plan for this new activity. Additional information in the chapter will primarily focus on the information needed for financial planning and the systems needed to sustain the operation.

For-profit and not-for-profit business plans are similar. However there are some important differences. The most significant difference is for-profits may have investors. Not-for-profits, on the other hand, have funders.

A for-profit organization, whether a sole proprietorship, partnership or corporation, exists primarily to generate a profit or to take in more money than it spends. The owners can decide to keep the profit or spend it on the business. Tax-exempt not-for-profit organizations exist to provide a service to the public and operate under rules that forbid the distribution of profits to owners. Additional information about for-profit and not-for-profit legal differences should be discussed with your lawyer, especially if you are just starting your day camp and are not operating under another organization.

Your plan's objectives and elements

A business plan helps you secure financing or sponsorship. It also forces you through a critical thinking process you'll need to move your program and meet the challenges that lie ahead. The Day Camp Business Plan outlined in Figure 4.1 provides the key checkpoints for a day camp business plan that would support a camp start-up. Note that if you are using your business plan as a part of a fund-raising proposal, you may need to adjust this format to meet the specific requirements of your funders.

Figure 4.1

Day Camp Business Plan

1. Executive Summary
- Generally a one- or two-page summary that highlights the proposed business, market, management, and financial forecasts

2. Mission and Outcomes
- Statement of purpose
- Youth development outcomes

3. Type of Business
- Resident, day, trip or travel camp, or combination

4. Ownership
- Business status: new business, existing business, takeover/buyout
- For-profit: individual proprietorship, partnership, corporation, shareholders
- Not-for-profit: agency, religious group, independent, public or governmental entity

5. Financial Objectives
- Profit, investors, planned subsidy, or break-even operation

6. Location and Facilities
- Desired location
- Environment and facilities
- Season(s) of operation
- Owned, rented, or leased facilities and/or equipment

7. Program Services Description
- Desired client outcomes or benefits
- Program structure and activities
- Projected number of campers per session
- Season and/or session length

8. Market Analysis
- Target clientele to be served
- Industry analysis and standards
- Competitive position
- Marketing plan

9. Management Plan
- Key individuals and duties, including board of directors, if applicable
- Administrative, support services, and program personnel plan
- Insurance and benefits
- Office and technology requirements
- Timetable

10. Start-up Costs
- Working capital available
- Capital investment required
- Consultants and/or personnel
- Legal fees
- Analysis of federal, state, county, municipal regulations and taxes required to operate
- Risk analysis and insurance
- Program, office, and other non-capitalized supplies and equipment
- Available collaborations or partnerships

11. Annual Budget
- Fee or tuition
- Other income sources
- Fixed and variable expenses
- Projected profit or loss

12. Cash flows Projections
- Monthly income and expenses
- Annual — three- to five-year projections

Budget as a Management Tool

Your budget is a carefully prepared statement designed to:

1. reflect the realistic expectations of income and expenses based on strategic plan and desired outcomes;
2. project income and expenditures of any given operation or program for a set time period;
3. monitor income and expenditures; and
4. evaluate accomplishments at the end of a period.

Fiscal policies and procedures ensure that good budget management:

1. provides a statement of the financial resources;
2. informs all concerned of the revenue available;
3. provides control of all funds;
4. offers guarantee of equitable distribution to all operations;
5. gives clear indication of the cost of various programs and services;
6. provides support for future revisions and appropriations; and
7. ensures most effective use of personnel, facilities, supplies, and equipment in accomplishing the camp's mission and desired outcomes.

Planning your budget

As anyone knows who's put one together, a budget is about more than just numbers. A budget is a planning tool, a guide, a measuring stick and report card for your program, all in a single package. It also can be a prime indicator and measurement of your camp's overall success or failure.

Budgeting for your day camp simply involves weighing what it is you would like to do—your program and activities—against your available financial and community resources. Your budget should act as a link between your program and budget realities. And, like all operational aspects of your camp, *it should also solidly support your outcomes.*

Your budget helps you map your financial outlook and define your program's direction and emphasis. After all, nothing better indicates our priorities in a given area than how we spend money to support them.

In its simplest terms, a budget is a yearly financial plan, one that reflects your desired outcomes and priorities. As such, it must be a living, vital document, one that you'll need to revisit annually and monitor on a monthly basis to keep current.

If your committee, board, or supervisor requires you to submit periodic reports, remember the twelve-month cycle, or fiscal year, may or may not be based on the calendar year. Find out what your supervisor requires and tailor your report submitting to those requirements. Also, if yours is an existing day camp, don't forget to factor in the changing requirements of your program. Remember to find out if there will there be new projects, more kids, or additional field trips. If your camp is new, be sure that you consider all of your costs and budget accordingly.

Most major income and expenses in day camps occur in a very short period of time, usually late spring and early summer. Even if you have an accounting department that takes care of logging income and paying bills, its reports may be a month behind your actual expenditures. To know where you are financially on a daily basis, keep a record of transactions that occur frequently such as purchases of food and medical supplies. There are a number of simple computer accounting systems available that enable you to keep track of your entire budget, or that specifically pertain to frequently used account numbers. The following information will help you better understand the key concepts behind the camp budgeting process.

There are several basic accounting practices and terms you will need to be familiar with. These include "direct costs" and "indirect costs," "fixed costs" and "variable costs," and "cash flows." The steps of basic accounting practices and related key terms are covered below.

Budgeting accounting practices:
- Establish a budget
- Document all income
- Deposit money promptly
- Establish controls on expenditures
- Pay approved invoices by check
- Establish a system of regular financial reports
- Plan for cash flows
- Plan for external annual audit

Budgeting terms:
- **Direct Costs** — costs related to food, program, staff, etc.
- **Indirect Costs** — costs related to central office space not on campsite, telephone, supervisor's time, etc.
- **Fixed Costs** — costs related to printing the brochure, property insurance, director's salary, etc.
- **Variable Costs** — costs related to program supplies, transportation, seasonal staff, etc.
- **Cash Flows** — income received and expenses paid in the same period of time.

As you begin putting your budget together, understand the difference between fixed and variable costs. As mentioned earlier, fixed costs are costs associated with expenditures that are fixed, or do not change as the number of campers or staff, or the number of camper-days change. Variable costs are those that change as you add more campers, staff and/or camper days.

It is helpful to note that direct and indirect costs are used primarily in not-for-profits. Indirect costs are usually those associated with administrative or overhead.

A yearly cash flows chart with projected income and expenses (by month) can help you plan for those times when there are cash shortages and overages.

Look at the sample budget format in Figure 4.2.

The percentage of income or expenses in each line item will vary depending on your plan. This example gives you an idea of what items are included in a budget. Some major considerations will be whether you have volunteer or paid staff, and if you furnish the transportation. The account numbers will depend on your organization's accounting system. Review the budget line items, check to see if it covers all the items in your plan or how it compares to a budget you may already have from your supervisor and/or the board of directors.

Once you have a concept of what the budget should look like, then you can begin to put the numbers to your plan.

Generally, in putting together a budget a good rule-of-thumb is to start with expenses. Start with what you want to *do*—not what you want to *charge*. Determine how many staff will you need, for how many hours, with what supplies, at what cost, and so on. Some people would say that this is the hard part, especially if you are starting without any history. It takes time and focus, but good record-keeping will make it easier next year.

Revenue

Revenue is income from fees, donations, grants, and other sources. You must have revenue prior to paying expenses. The simplest method of determining your day camp fee is by dividing a reasonable number of expected campers by your total expenses.

In determining fees, consider whether you plan to make a profit, break even, or subsidize your program. In Figure 4.3 the graph shows day camp fee ranges for ACA-accredited camps. Black indicates fees for independent for-profit camps and grey for not-for-profits. Note: this graph does not reflect any donations or other subsidies to a program.

A budget is a guide or map. Be sure that you are as accurate in your budget predictions as possible. Also try to be responsive when your staff explains the reasons they need something that will necessitate budget revisions.

Be honest about your budget, it will be a key guide throughout the season as you make important decisions about your camp. Much of the budgeting process is a process of give-and-take; for this reason, making your needs known, and evaluating these needs against available resources in the agency and/or community, are a key part of the budgeting process.

Budget/Chart of Accounts

Figure 4.2

Acct.	Revenue/Income	Fixed	Variable	Total Budget
110	Tuition/Fees			
	# __ participants x $ __ x __sessions			
120	Program/Activity Fees			
	# __ participants x $ __ x __sessions			
122	Transportation Fees			
	# __ participants x $ __ x __sessions			
130	Rentals User Group Income			
140	Sales (camp store, meals)			
150	Contributions/Subsidy			
160	Miscellaneous			
	Total Income			

Expenses

Acct.		Fixed	Variable	Total Budget
200	Wages			
	Year-round			
	Seasonal			
230	Taxes and Benefits			
300	Food and Related			
400	Occupancy (utilities) or Building Use Fees			
420	Maintenance/Repairs/Depreciation			
430	Equipment Purchase			
450	Property Taxes			
460	Property/Liability/Medical Insurance			
500	Transportation (camper)			
	# buses/veh. rented __ x $ __ x __ days/weeks			
600	Program			
	Supplies			
	Contract fees or admissions			
700	Training/Conferences			
710	Dues, Fees			
740	Training/Staff Travel			
800	Office			
810	Postage			
820	Supplies			
840	Marketing			
900	Board/Committee			
1000	Miscellaneous/Indirect			
	Total Expenses			

ACA-Accredited Day Camps

Figure 4.3

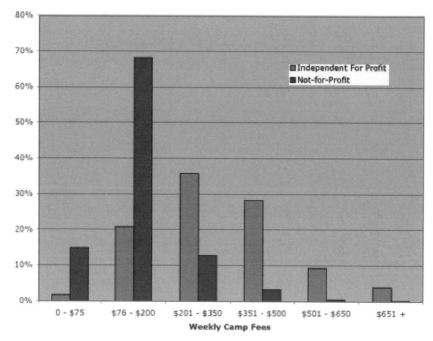

Money and resources are not always available to do all of the things in your plan. The good news is a creative, solutions-focused approach to your program can often make up for budget shortfalls. For example, have printed materials donated, encourage volunteers to donate time for labeling and placing postage on brochures, invite volunteers to run display booths, have older youth from a current program help with a letter writing campaign. Get a business to pay for refreshments at open house or other promotional events.

A budget is a measurement of success. Your approved budget will be an important measurement tool for your day camp. The budget tells you, your supervisor, your board and your funders how well you are planning and how well you are achieving your plans. Weekly results need to be compared with the plan. Is the plan on track? Doing better than expected? Not doing as well? What adjustments need to be made? It is important that problems are identified as early as possible so that corrections can be made. Budgets are often used as a tool in the evaluation process and may also be taken into account when considering future pay increases.

How does your budget contribute to your outcomes? You must have the resources available to accomplish everything that you have planned to do at your day camp. Think back to Chapter 1, where you developed specific outcomes: Considering an outcome of individual skill-building with archery as the method.

Would you be successful at achieving it if you only had enough equipment for the campers to wait in line to shoot one time? Could you achieve it without a trained instructor? What other ways could you achieve this outcome if there was limited or no money budgeted for equipment or certification of a specialist?

Funding success

Managing the money that funds your camp's operation through good planning and realistic budgets is, in many ways, as important as the money itself. After all, funding—and how you manage it—will, to a large degree, determine your camp program's success.

For this reason, it is essential that you equip your camp with the processes and tools that will enable you to build and maintain the kind of business-viable operation that any great camp program deserves.

"As you start to put your budget together, work on your expenses first; that will tell you what you need revenue-wise. Once you do your expenses and revenue, you can see if your revenue is adequate. I look at my revenue and say, 'I need to bring in 160 campers to provide the revenue that will cover these expenses.' Knowing that I an realistically only get 150 campers, I have to either adjust my revenue (increase the fee or recruit more campers) or cut my expenses."
–Chris Winkler, YMCA Camp Eagle Rock, Charlotte, North Carolina.

Courtesy of Camp Mondamin/M.E. Bailey, Tuxedo, North Carolina

Chapter 5

The Inner-workings— Your Administration

You've got your program together. Now, let's get to work organizing your administration—the processes and staff that will enable you to bring your program to life.

If your program is the "heart and soul" of your camp, your administration is its "arms and legs." As such, it must be an essential focus in your overall camp planning. Your program, no mater how life-changing it has the potential to be, will be seriously handicapped if it lacks the administrative structure or resources it needs to make it viable.

A good camp administration calls for building into your program the kind of proven administrative practices that are essential to ensuring customer satisfaction, "making your numbers," seeing to it your camp operates efficiently, and other goals. Good administration also can help you in less obvious ways, such as making your camp the kind of efficient and orderly place your staff wants to work—a key component in attracting and retaining quality staff.

How you manage the day-to-day details of your camp also plays a part in supporting your outcomes. In fact, some veteran camp directors will tell you that no single factor of camp operation is as important to a camp's "higher mission" than a good administration. After all, a camp is only as good as it is effective; and a camp can only be effective in fulfilling its mission if it's *effectively run*.

Beginning to design your administration

Of course, as camp director, you will play an essential role in your camp's administrative structure. You will serve an essential coordinating function between many groups and individuals affiliated with the camp, including your organization or camp board, (if you have one) staff, customers, (children and parents), the community . . . even the media. As director, you will have primary responsibility over many areas. You'll also be the most visible representative of your camp to the community.

It goes without saying that you'll be busy. But not as busy as you'd be if your camp lacked a good, workable administrative structure. Want to learn how frustrating and time-consuming running a day camp can be? Just try heading up a camp that is poorly run or managed. That's why you'll need to draw on your very best planning skills as you put together your camp team and processes.

While your role in your camp's administration will be significant, you won't be going it alone. Camp administration, by its very nature, is *team-based*. For this reason, the sooner you learn an important operating principle of good camp management, the faster you'll be on the road to mapping out a good administrative structure.

Ready? Here it is: *Know your job and do it well. And make sure your staff does the same.*

Assigning roles and responsibilities

As camp director, some administrative and operational duties will fall squarely on your shoulders. These may include ensuring that your program adheres to your mission and outcomes, maintaining health and safety and other operational standards, and overseeing legal-related and other issues.

Other roles and responsibilities you'll be able to assign to your staff. Still others you'll manage together. So, how do you decide who does what? The next couple of exercises can help. Let's start with defining the roles and responsibilities of the members of your camp staff.

First, let's look at inventorying and assigning your camp responsibilities. (If you don't yet have a staff, you can assign responsibilities to "a position yet to be filled.")

Figure 5.1 shows one way to document the day camp administrative responsibilities for your camp.

As a first step in completing the form, meet with your team of camp decision makers (backing organization, governing board, camp committee and, if available, legal counsel). The advice and counsel of these important camp partners can give you

Day Camp Administrative Responsibilities

In addition to individuals who provide direct program services, who else carries responsibilities for day camp administration? Check all the positions that are a part of your responsibilities. Identify others in your organization who have some responsibility for day camp and their supervisors.

Figure 5.1

✓ Your tasks	Positions	Name or Initials	Specific Responsiblities Related to Day Camp	Responsible to
	Executive Director			
	Director of Program Services			
	Day Camp Administrator			
	On-site Day Camp Director			
	Bookkeeper			
	Registrar			
	Secretary			
	Personnel Director			
	Site Manager			
	Web Site Director			
	Production Services			
	Public Relations Director			
	Receptionist			
	Purchasing			

valuable input and insights as you go about the important task of clearly outlining and documenting roles and responsibilities. (It's also a good way to build and strengthen a solid team relationship, build an operational consensus, and keep your camp aligned with organizational goals and program outcomes.)

Now, back to the chart. If your camp already has a staff, take a crack at assigning duties. In the "Responsible to" category, be sure to note who reports to whom. This will later help you define the overall reporting structure of your staff.

It's easier to complete the form if you have clear and accurate job descriptions for each member of your staff. If you don't, let's look at one way you can put them together.

Crafting your camp's job descriptions

If job descriptions already exist at your camp, you'll want to review and update them prior to each camp season. If you need to create them, the exercise below can help you get started.

In addition to helping you appropriately assign administrative tasks, clearly written, accurate job descriptions can assist you during staff hiring. Good job descriptions can better enable you to target your hires and hire *strategically*. (We will cover staff hiring and retention later in this chapter.)

Your staff will play essential roles in virtually every aspect of your camp—from your ability to achieve your outcomes, to ensuring customer satisfaction, to getting along with your campers. For this reason, begin the important work of putting together a quality staff by developing good job descriptions.

Developing job descriptions: a how-to

While there are a number of different job description formats, most include the following elements. (The sequence of these elements, however, may slightly differ.):

- Job title
- Responsible to
- Minimum qualifications
- Camp goals or youth development outcomes
- General staff responsibilities
- Specific job responsibilities
- Essential functions

Minimum qualifications are required qualifications a staff member will need to apply for the position. These may include special training, skills, certifications, and general qualifications required of all staff.

Responsibilities are divided into *general* responsibilities for all staff, and those *specific to the position.*

Figure 5.2 is a sample of a counselor's job description.

Day Camp Counselor Job Description

Responsible to: Head Counselor/Unit Leader

Minimum Qualifications:
- ✓ Desire and ability to work with children outdoors.
- ✓ Ability to relate to one's peer group.
- ✓ Ability to accept supervision and guidance.
- ✓ Good character, integrity, and adaptability.
- ✓ High school graduate or equivalent, or at least 18 years of age.
- ✓ Enthusiasm, sense of humor, patience, and self-control.
- ✓ Experience as a camper and/or experience working with children.

Responsibility for Camp's Youth Development Outcomes:
- ✓ Commitment and desire to help the camp achieve the following outcomes for campers: (List your camp's specific outcomes)

Specific Job Responsibilities:
- ✓ Assume responsibility for the health and welfare of campers entrusted to his/her care.
- ✓ Help each participant achieve the desired outcomes for camper development.
- ✓ Provide opportunities for the campers to participate successfully in all aspects of the camp experience.
- ✓ Identify and meet individual camper needs.
- ✓ Recognize and provide opportunities for group interaction, problem solving, and decision making.
- ✓ Guide group or individuals in activity plans.
- ✓ Carry out established roles in enforcing camp safety regulations and implementing emergency procedures.
- ✓ Supervise all assigned aspects of the campers' day including arrival and departure, meal times, and rest times.

Figure 5.2

Continued on next page...

Figure 5.2

✓ Assist in teaching or leading activities, as assigned.

✓ Participate in the camper individual evaluation process as requested.

General Responsibilities for All Staff:

✓ Prepare for and actively participate in staff training, meetings, and supervisory conferences.

✓ Set a good example for campers and others including cleanliness, punctuality, personal language, appearance, health habits, sportsmanship, and manners.

✓ Adhere to the camp's personnel policies.

✓ Encourage respect for personal property, camp equipment, and facilities.

✓ Maintain good public relations with campers' parents and the neighboring community.

✓ Submit all required reports on time.

✓ Assist in maintaining a positive physical environment during opening, camper sessions, and closing of camp.

✓ Evaluate the current season and make recommendations for equipment, supplies, and programs for the following season.

✓ These are not the only duties to be preformed. Some duties may be reassigned and other duties may be assigned as required.

Essential Functions:

✓ Be physically able to accompany the campers to any of the camp activities.

✓ Cognitive and communications ability to plan and conduct the activity to achieve camper development outcomes.

✓ Be able to communicate verbally with campers and provide instruction.

✓ Have visual ability to recognize hazards in the camp setting as well as physical symptoms of camper injury or illness.

✓ Have auditory ability to respond appropriately to hazards and any camper concerns.

✓ Be able to observe camper behavior in daily camp life, assess its appropriateness, enforce appropriate safety regulations and emergency procedures, and apply appropriate behavior management techniques.

Courtesy of Camp Laurel, Lebanon, Connecticut

Putting together your planning template

Your camp's planning template is your administrative plan. The planning template lets you identify, in one or two pages, the many and varied tasks of running a camp. It also helps you prioritize them and assign a timeline for task completion. Together with another valuable planning tool, the sample "Yearly Work Calendar," the planning template offers a quick and easy way to organize the many administrative details and tasks of running a camp.

Figure 5.3 shows a standard day camp planning template. This template is on the CD-ROM that accompanies this book.

Figure 5.3

Planning Template for

_____ **Day Camp**

Before*	Task	Responsibility
	Select on-site director	
	Decide on outcomes for participants	
	Determine target population	
	Decide on program activities	
	Decide on program structure	
	Decide on field trips	
	Design schedule for the day/week	
	Arrange transportation services	
	Decide on lunches and snacks (how provided)	
	Design business plan and budget	
	Set fees	
	Design campership program	
	Set dates	
	Design staff structure and organization	
	Write job descriptions	
	Decide on themes	
	Design staff screening system	
	Produce staff recruitment materials	
	Select location	
	Produce camper recruitment materials	
	Set up registration system	

*(date for completion)

Before*	Task	Responsibility
	Create a risk management plan	
	Obtain insurance	
	Review and utilize ACA standards for planning; take ACA standards course	
	Purchase supplies	
	Train and screen drivers	
	Secure equipment	
	Write emergency procedures	
	Arrange for emergency services	
	Select a media spokesperson	
	Arrange for site and grounds maintenance	
	Arrange for trash pick-up	
	Communicate transportation arrangements	
	Recruit and hire staff	
	Send follow-up information to staff	
	Do background checks — driving, criminal records, child abuse	
	Produce staff manuals	
	Acquire any licenses and tests	
	Design arrival and release of campers	
	Allocate campership funds	
	Decide on any awards or recognition	
	Produce forms for attendance, requisitions, etc.	
	Design staff training	
	Train staff	
	Arrange for storage of group supplies	
	Arrange for storage of personal items	
	Plan volunteer work days for set-up	
	Produce evaluation forms	
	Send follow-up information to campers	
	Set up petty cash	
	Secure first-aid supplies	
	Set up first-aid area	
	Arrange system for notification of cancellation	
	Arrange staff participation in ACA training	
	Post emergency phone numbers	
	Prepare facilities — fire extinguishers checked, smoke detector batteries, etc.	

*(date for completion)

continued on next page...

Before*	Task	Responsibility
	Arrange camper groups	
	Respond to parent needs/concerns	
	Supervise safe loading and unloading of buses/vehicles	
	Supervise staff — document staff observations	
	On-going inspection of site for hazards	
	Communicate special needs or diets	
	Take photos	
	Visit program sites regularly	
	Plan and publicize volunteer work days for closing	
	Pay bills and payroll	
	Settle any outstanding bills	
	Compile participation data	
	Secure any post-camp evaluations	
	Prepare report for sponsoring organization	
	Follow-up on any insurance claims	
	Supervise volunteer work day for closing	
	Review policies	
	File records for designated time	
	Review programs from summer	
	Write thank you letters	
	Inventory and store supplies and equipment	

Figure 5.3

*(date for completion)

Begin by reviewing the operational tasks on the CD-ROM template. If you're working in an existing camp, these may be already compiled. If not, work with your experienced staff to identify tasks. If you're starting from scratch in a new camp, compile as many tasks as you can think of, adding others as you uncover them during your planning. Also, feel free to pull tasks from the sample Yearly Calendar. The chart lists many administrative tasks that day camps commonly share.

Now it's time to prioritize your tasks. Fill in a completion date, and reorder the list in chronological order. Now, with first things first, assign responsibility for the task. (Don't hesitate to review your job descriptions again if you need more clarification about who in your staff is appropriate for the job.)

Your yearly work calendar/checklist

A sample yearly work calendar/checklist will give you ideas for your planning template. It is formatted as a simple calendar-based checklist, and designed to help you easily check off those tasks you add to your planning template month-by-month. It also helps you customize your yearly work calendar with months and person responsible. (Find a customizable version for use at your camp on your CD-ROM.)

Figure 5.4 shows the sample of a yearly work calendar/checklist.

Day Camp Director/Administrator
Yearly Work Calendar/Checklist

Figure 5.4

The following checklist is a guide to tasks that a camp director needs to accomplish. Because the staffing, program, season of operation, size, fiscal year, type of camp, etc., will differ with each camp, the exact month or task may need to be adjusted to fit the unique circumstances of the camp operation.

September
- evaluate previous season
- compile staff evaluation results
- review equipment inventory and assess needed repairs
- begin or determine status of strategic plan including setting or revising outcomes
- begin or review success of business plan
- review programs and program operational plans from summer
- determine ratios for each program area and groups
- communicate site needs to site manager and/or camp committee
- review and evaluate policies, standards, legal obligations
- turn in all invoices and ensure that bills have been paid
- update budget with projected expenses
- compile participation data
- compile medical data, label and store health records
- follow-up on insurance claims
- compare attendance figures with previous year and national trends
- catalog photos for promotional purposes

continued on next page...

Figure 5.4

October
- set camp dates including pre-camp
- compile camper/parent evaluations/survey
- determine program activities and certifications needed, including first aid
- design program structure with outcomes, progression and balance in mind
- determine staff ratio
- determine staff positions/staff organization

November
- design or review job descriptions
- update personnel policies, contracts, application forms
- design staff recruitment/screening plan
- set camp fees
- finalize budget
- determine special themes or sessions
- design camper recruitment plan and target population
- design marketing plan
- determine camp brochure content
- place camp information/schedule in newsletters and announce dates to returning campers
- develop teaser promotional flyer

December
- design/revise registration system
- letter to returning staff w/application
- staff event/reunion
- contract with transportation services and arrange pick-up locations
- design and complete camp brochure
- camp brochure to printer
- register for ACA standards course if accreditation visit is next summer
- finalize camper registration system and train personnel

January
- solicit campership funds
- design campership applications
- reserve site (lease/rental)
- renew necessary licenses
- review program plans
- continue staff recruitment
- design supervision systems and accountability
- set up or secure resources for water safety and first-aid training

- design/review risk management plan
- review camp policies including those on sexual harassment and child abuse
- review state and federal law on employment
- provide tax information to IRS and W-4 forms to previous year's staff contact for international counselors
- prepare information/display for job fairs

February
- set up and conduct staff interviews
- conduct background and reference checks
- provide additional camp information for newsletters
- design follow-up information to registered campers: medicals, what to bring, maps, etc.
- order program supplies

March
- determine content for staff training
- complete application for first-time ACA accreditation by March first
- acquire state certification/license as required
- set up camp bookkeeping system
- solicit campership funds
- conduct pre-camp maintenance inspection
- purchase or replace equipment
- review supply of forms for camp including cookouts, awards, inventory, petty cash, etc.
- prepare ads for last-minute staff recruitment
- review insurance plans for workers' compensation, medical, liability, fire, etc., and secure forms
- check compliance with ACA standards and prepare information for accreditation visit

April
- order camp awards/recognition items
- review status of camper registration
- compile/develop staff training materials
- contact resource people for staff training
- finalize contracts for special programs, field trips, etc.
- meet with suppliers for pre-camp purchasing: supplies, etc.
- check goals and system for registration

continued on next page...

Figure 5.4

- distribute brochures to doctors' offices, corporations, etc.
- set up promotional events
- site visit for hazard identification
- set up fire-fighting equipment
- recharge fire extinguishers
- contact authorities for inspections
- arrange for trash pick-up
- develop staff manual
- arrange for camp medical services
- plan for camper daily check-in and checkout
- design/review counselor-in-training or day camp aide programs

May

- secure I-9 and W-4 forms for staff to fill out
- review status of camper registration
- allocate campership funds
- revise/design camper evaluation
- attend volunteer work days
- work with site manager to prepare roads, etc.
- review OSHA regulations, i.e., hazardous waste, lockout/tagout, Material Safety Data Sheets (MSDS), accident reports, etc.
- notification of operations (fire, police, etc.)
- have phones turned on
- set up kitchen, office, infirmary, etc.
- set up living facilities
- stock program areas
- finish and compile staff manual
- apply for camper/staff health and accident insurance
- check fee balances paid
- plan and promote camp open house
- finalize camp program
- survey staff to plan for training (staff needs assessment)
- plan for pre-camp training
- discuss staff expectations and assess staff strengths for training and assignments
- coordinate director and staff needs for training
- finalize risk management plan
- order medical supplies and medical log books
- arrange for emergency medical treatment
- plan for dispensing medication
- finalize program or other contracts
- design transportation/pick-up routes

- secure adult supervision for vehicles
- arrange for emergency transportation
- have water tested
- enroll staff in certification courses, i.e., first aid, lifeguard, OLS, archery, etc.

June, July, August
- have staff complete I-9 and W-4 forms
- conduct pre-camp training for staff
- set up waterfront and/or other program areas and staff
- assign staff to units
- plan for weather effects on program
- implement risk management plan
- review camper registration information
- arrange for staff meetings
- arrange for staff time off
- arrange for in-service training
- design and arrange on-site purchasing
- design and arrange on-site bookkeeping
- handle budget administration/revision
- hold camp open house
- invite board and/or committee to camp
- display required government posters
- post rules and regulations
- post emergency phone numbers
- arrange for inspection/visitation tours (i.e., inspectors, parents, ACA, etc.)
- design kaper charts and assignments
- conduct health screening for campers and staff
- implement check-in and checkout systems for campers
- implement camper planning opportunities
- take video, slides, and photographs for brochures and promotion
- handle and document camper behavior problems
- be prepared to handle or delegate communication with parents during camp
- have on-going evaluation at end of each session with campers and staff
- design staff evaluation for end of season
- give positive reinforcement to staff
- establish delivery days
- communicate with cook and/or staff regarding campers' allergies and special needs

continued on next page...

Figure 5.4

- review health forms with nurse
- assign campers to groups
- plan special theme programs, closing campfires, flag ceremonies, etc.
- physically survey all areas of camp periodically for maintenance problems, hazards, staff or camper problems, etc.
- handle any emergencies, complete incident reports, and process insurance claims
- practice emergency drills
- conduct pre- and post-season inventories of equipment and supplies

August

- hold staff performance evaluations including discussion of job functions, reporting structure, interests for next summer, suggested changes, etc.
- arrange for storage of equipment and supplies

On-going and constant tasks and responsibilities

- interpret mission and youth development outcomes of camp
- budget revisions
- allocation of funds for emergency repairs
- apply for grants
- process accounts receivables and accounts payables
- secure necessary board approval for policy and budget changes
- set up procedures for user groups that rent or lease the facility
- set up procedures for short-term programs and offer appropriate training to leaders
- camp promotional presentations
- maintain parent contacts
- recruit volunteers for involvement in planning
- provide support for volunteers
- review and utilize ACA standards for planning
- participate in ACA national and regional conferences, section education events and/or participate in other professional development, training, and networking opportunities

Your yearly work calendar/planning template is a simple, yet valuable tool. It is an excellent way to manage your administrative details—and make sure essential tasks get done, not dropped between the cracks. The flexibility of the version on your CD allows you to alter the order of your tasks and rank them under whatever month you choose.

Get ready to sign up: the registration process

Of course, there is much, much more to the camp registration process than just having a camper or parent fill out and sign a form. Far from being a simple formality, registration is not only a fairly involved administrative system, it is the process through which your customers start their formal relationship with your camp. Indeed, it may be the *first* interaction your campers and their families have with you and your staff. As you know, first impressions are everything, so when it comes to registration you'll want to do it right.

Here are some items you'll want to be thinking about as you begin planning your registration process:

- What forms will you need?
- What information should be included on the forms?
- Will you register campers online, by phone or fax, or only by completed paper form? If other than in person or by mail, how will you secure parent/guardian signature? Note: make sure your form is faxable (black or blue ink on white paper).
- How will you handle payment? (check, credit card, cash?)
- Will you be registering individual campers, or groups?
- What permissions/waivers must you obtain?
- Who in your staff will process the registrations? (Consult your planning template.)
- Who will train the registrar to answer parents' questions about camp?
- How will you handle money?
- When will you start taking registrations?
- Will you place limits on the number of campers? Age groups served? Type of programs?
- How will you handle cancellations? Do you have a refund policy? What is it?
- What information will you send campers to confirm their registration?

Figure 5.5 provides a sample of a Camper Registration Form. (A modifiable version can be found on your CD-ROM.)

Your camp registration form brings to you information that will be important to your camp in several ways. First and foremost, it gives you the necessary information to enroll the camper in a way that's in conformity with legal and regulatory policies. It also serves as the information source for your camp's database. This database will be a vital resource to you, especially as you begin your marketing or competitive benchmarking. For this reason, you'll want to design your registration form to collect all the information you need and in a sequence that simplifies entering the information in your database.

Figure 5.5

For Office Use Only
Date Registration Received:
Section assigned:
Entered Database ☐ Confirmation mailed
Total fee
Deposit paid
Credit
Balance due
Balance paid

Day Camp Registration

Camper's Name:

Last _____First _____

Address _____

City _____

State _____ Zip _____

Home Phone _____

Cell Phone _____

Age _____ M/F _____ Date of Birth _____

Grade in Fall _____

Custodial Parent(s)/Guardian:

Name _____

Day Phone_____ Evening Phone _____

Name _____

Day Phone_____ Evening Phone _____

Note: Please circle preferred parent or guardian to contact during camp:

My child is in the custodial care of (check one): ☐ both parents

❑ mother only   ❑ father only   ❑ other _____

May your child be released to anyone other than the custodial

parent/guardian? ❑ yes   ❑ no

If yes, please list: _____

Emergency contact if parents cannot be reached:

Name _____

Day Phone _____

Evening Phone_____

Cell Phone _____

Check enclosed payable to: xxx

Charge $_____ ❑ Visa ❑ MC ❑ Other:_____

Name as it appears on card _____

Address for card billing _____

Account number _____

exp. date _____

Signature on card _____

Other information:

Camper has been to day camp before: ❑ yes   ❑ no

Session(s) 1ˢᵗ Choice _____

Session(s) 2ⁿᵈ Choice _____

We learned about day camp from: _____

Transportation:

(Request transportation information needed. Choice of bus stop, etc.)

Program:

(Request any program choices needed.)

Other:

(T-shirt size, camp buddy name, registered as organization member, troop name or number, etc.)

I have read the camp information and understand the nature of the activities and the health and safety measures. I give permission for my child to attend and participate in activities on and off the camp property. I give permission for my child to be photographed/videotaped and for the camp to use the pictures for publicity purposes. I understand and agree to cooperate with all regulations and procedures.

Parent/guardian signature_____Date _____

Mail to:
Registrar
XYZ
1234 Street
Anytown, USA
Fax (xxx) xxx xxxx

You'll also want to make sure your registration process captures information about camper health coverage. (Other health and safety issues will be covered in detail in Chapter 7.)

Consider using one of ACA's business partners for registration-related services. These businesses can provide valuable support in key areas, including software and online camp registration solutions—from early registration to activities selection, payment processing, and management reports; or they can set up your own system.

As you prepare your registation processes:

- Put together a database that enables the registration of children by age categories or special programs they wish to participate in. Log data in the database and on the registration form. In the database, you will want to have fields that tally the number of campers in each age category and on the waiting list.
- Then make columns for date registered, child's name, parent's or guardian's name, address, phone, special program, amount paid, balance due and transportation needs. Add pre/post camp participation for those participating in extended day programs.
- Process payment (system should be set up to process cash and checks and/or credit cards) and send the parent a confirmation packet.
- Copy registration form and maintain one copy in the office and send one to camp. By keeping track of the date registered, next year you will be able to see if you are ahead or behind registration at the same time the previous year.

On most databases you can rearrange the list by registration date, age, alphabetical name, program, bus stop, etc. for various purposes including forming groups or making bus lists. Some camps leave a blank column for the director for special notes on the child the parent has shared. You might want to add the name of the person who has permission to pick up the child each day.

Staffing for success

If you ask anyone in business to name his or her single most important asset, chances are the answer you'll get will be, "My people." Those who run day camps will tell you the same thing. No other factor—your program, location of your camp, or size of your budget—plays as important a role in your success as your staff.

Your staff puts a face and personality to your program and camp. For your campers your staff is the first line of interaction between themselves and your program. They play an *absolutely essential* role in the success of your camp.

The bad news is what many camp directors admit: recruiting and keeping committed, enthusiastic, and qualified staff present the biggest challenges the camping industry faces. For this reason, you'll need to put much thought, time, and resources into how you attract, hire, and retain the gifted staff your program deserves.

The first step involves deciding what specific staff positions you'll need and how many staff members you'll have to hire to fill them.

You know approximately how many campers you'll be serving. Your program, including activities and scheduling, is in place. You've identified your key administrative staff needs through your evaluation of camp administrative responsibilities. In Chapter 2 we looked at some suggested staff/camper ratios. The next step is taking a comprehensive look at your camp to determine your staffing requirements, including supervision.

Figure 5.6 (a) lists some of the key factors that should figure into your staffing equation.

You'll notice in the example, the secondary chart 5.6 (a) (Sample On-site Staff Organization) gives you the opportunity to begin fleshing out your staffing needs in accordance with the staffing factors noted in the rest of the chart. After you've reviewed the staff organizations that the chart provides for small and large day camps, try your hand at designing a staff for a mid-size camp. Now try to determine what you need for your camp.

"Staffing is the lifeblood of our camp. We have wonderful facilities. We have climbing towers, pools, fishing. But the one thing that's going to make the camp work for the camper is his or her experience with the counselor. That relationship between camper and counselor is essential, because later that camper will not remember just swimming: he or she will remember swimming with their counselor. Good staff is critical."
—Chris Winkler, YMCA Camp Eagle Rock Charlotte, North Carolina

On-site Staffing Factors

Figure 5.6 (a)

Factors	Small Day Camp	Mid-Size Day Camp	Large Day Camp
Number of campers	50 or fewer campers	150 campers	350 campers
Activities	No activities that require special skills or certifications	Two activities that require special skills or certifications	Six activities that require special skills or certifications
Site	Small city park, easily observed, picnic tables and one open shelter	Wooded area, pool, central lodge and shelters, first-aid tent	Large acreage, public lake, central lodge with kitchen, archery range, challenge course, sports fields, nature, and craft areas
Meals	Sack lunch	Small kitchen with refrigeration and some cookouts	Kitchen, sack lunch, some served cold or hot lunches
Transportation	Parent-arranged	Some parent, some vans or buses	Primarily contracted bus service
Length of day	9 to 3	8:30 to 3:30 with extended day option	8:30 to 3:30 with extended day option
Length of session	One week	One week	One to 4 weeks

Sample On-site Staff Organization

Figure 5.6 (b)

Small day camp	Mid-size day camp	Large day camp
On-site director • Assist. program director • First aider 6 counselors		On-site director • Assist. director • Program director • Business/office manager • Nurse • Food service manager, cook • 10 specialist director and/or leaders • 4 head counselors or unit ldrs. • 35 counselors Site manager

Courtesy of Camp Ho Mita Koda, Newbury, Ohio

Paid or volunteer staff?

Now that you've identified the positions you'll need to staff, let's determine which staff type, paid or volunteer, is best suited to fill them.

There'll be more behind this decision than just a financial consideration. Day camp offers a unique opportunity to blend paid and volunteer staff in ways that can bring an added scope and dimension to your program. Still, you'll need to determine if paid or volunteer staffing is best for each of your available positions.

Let's look at questions and an exercise that can help. First the questions:

- Will you offer multiple week-long sessions on different sites, or use one site for multiple weeks?
- Is your camp season one week, several weeks, or the entire summer?
- If you are planning multiple week-long sessions, do they follow each other, or are they spread out over the summer with a week or more between the sessions?

Armed with your answers, now think about the following situations:

- **You want to offer week-long day camps at multiple sites.** — Why might a different volunteer staff for each site be advantageous? Think about volunteers' willingness to drive to multiple sites, and how long volunteers are willing to give their time. Also, will they want to volunteer for a youth organization or church group they already work with on a regular basis?
- **You want to offer eight week-long day camp sessions on one site.** — Why might a paid staff be an advantage? Think about whether volunteer staff or paid staff are more qualified. Do paid staff members want short term or long-term employment? How does staff that change each week effect the training and supervision of a staff team and program consistency?
- **You'd like to consider international staff, or you're having trouble finding staff members who live a reasonable distance for daily commuting.** — What do you need to consider? Think about whether paid or volunteer staff would be best. What are other options are open in addition to commuting? What problems or advantages would these have?

As you weigh the advantages of paid or volunteer staff, ask: "What are the differences in the two screening processes?" Think about applications, interviews, references, criminal records checks, verification of work history, and so on.

As you work through these situations, you'll probably soon figure out that most volunteers are not willing to drive daily to sites, especially those far from their homes. In addition, you'll probably learn that most do not have the whole summer to give to your camp. You'll need to keep these factors in mind before you ask volunteer staff to handle too many of your staffing requirements.

Often the question arises, "Which is more qualified: paid or volunteer staff?" Here it is important to bear in mind that overall qualification depends on the individual. Volunteers are often just as qualified as paid staff; in fact, they may be more mature, given their age and experience.

It is easier, however, to build a staff team and provide training and supervision for a paid staff that will be with the camp for the entire summer. Other staffing alternatives to volunteers include international staff. International staff, or staff who prefer to live on-site rather than commute, can often be hired by providing on-site housing or housing with host families. Because high-school age staff are minors, the camp may assume more responsibility for their supervision on their time off, especially if these staff members are living on the site.

Whatever staffing option works best for you, remember that the screening process for all staff working with children (including returning staff) should be the same. When acquiring staff *you must be aware of key employment laws.*

Figure 5.7 is an overview of these laws. You may want to consult with your organization or legal counsel to have a better understanding of your legal obligations.

Federal Employment Laws and Regulations

Federal Employment Law	Enforcement Agency
Title VII (Civil Rights Act of 1964) prohibits discrimination on the basis of sex, race, religion, color or national origin. Also prohibits retaliation for filing a charge, testifying, etc. Civil Rights Act of 1991 expands remedies under Title VII and makes suits easier for plaintiffs alleging discrimination.	Equal Employment Opportunity Commission (EEOC) www.eeoc.gov
Age Discrimination in Employment Act (ADEA) prohibits discrimination on the basis of age (40 and over).	EEOC
National Child Protection Act of 1993 establishes a central computerized database of child abuse crime information. States are required to report arrests, convictions, and final dispositions of child abuse offenders.	States are encouraged, but not required to pass laws requiring child-care providers to obtain background checks on paid staff and volunteers.

Figure 5.7

continued on next page...

Federal Employment Law	Enforcement Agency
Fair Labor Standards Act regulates payment of wages and overtime requirements, etc.	Secretary of Labor
Occupational Safety and Health Act requires employers to provide workplaces free from recognized hazards to employees and requires employers to comply with occupational safety and health standards issued by OSHA. Requires employers to have programs for: (1) hazardous materials; (2) locking out/tagging out machinery; and (3) protecting employees from blood-borne diseases.	Occupational Safety & Health Administration (OSHA) www.osha.gov
Americans with Disabilities Act increases access to public accommodations for disabled persons and prohibits discrimination in employment on the basis of disability.	Department of Justice (Access) www.usdoj.gov/crt/ada/adahom1.htm EEOC (Employment)
Family and Medical Leave Act of 1993 provides employees with 12 weeks of unpaid leave for maternity, adoption, personal and family illness.	Secretary of Labor www.dol.gov/esa/regs/statutes/whd/ fmla.htm
Veterans protection/preference laws require employers to grant leave to employees for military service and return employees to work after military service. www.dol.gov/vets/programs/fact/vete rans_preference_fs08.htm	U.S. Attorney General

Figure 5.7

Courtesy of Crystal Lake Park District, Crystal Lake, Illinois

BEST staffing

The following acronym will help you remember four major staffing touch-stones:

B (bringing staff onboard)
E (ensuring staff remain)
S (strive for quality)
T (training goals)

Let's look at the role each of these plays in your program; first "bringing staff onboard."

Bringing staff onboard

Before you start inviting people in off the street to discuss employment opportunities at your camp, you'll need to make sure you've already covered important ground. Some areas we've already touched on; others we'll cover later in this chapter. To start, let's review:

- Identify the positions you'll need to fill; determine if they're paid or volunteer positions. Be sure to note any special qualifications (e.g., degrees, certifications, or training) the position may require.
- List responsibilities for each position.
- Define the reporting structure of these positions.
- Write or review job descriptions.
- Determine appropriate staffing levels given number of campers and program requirements.
- Determine compensation.
- Establish a staff screening and employment process (that you've approved with your organization, camp board and/or legal counsel).

Camp directors are quick to underscore how critical staff are to their programs. "Our most important outcome is promoting a family atmosphere," says Sandra Thompson, Recreation Supervisor of Crystal Lake Park District Day Camps in Crystal Lake, Illinois. "Good staff makes it possible to achieve that. Once we find a great staff member, we encourage them to recruit their friends. And we've found that some families just seem to produce great counselors—many times the siblings of great counselors also end up being excellent, so we actively recruit them as well.

"It's also important to have a logical progression in your structure; first campers become Junior Leaders, then Counselors, then Assistance Directors and finally Directors. Workers who come all the way through the ranks are often the best."

Ensuring staff remain—strive for quality

Good staff is hard to get. This is especially true for seasonal staff. For this reason, it is important that you recognize the value your staff brings to your camp and do what you can to retain them. You have invested in the time and money to recruit and train them; they have experience in your camp and know what you expect. Retaining staff is largely dependent on how they feel about the job they did and how they were treated.

Understand that your staff members have a life outside of camp and sometimes need to attend to things like weddings, funerals, or other family requirements. Set-up requirements for how they should request personal days.

Be concerned about the health and energy of your staff members. If they are overworked or tired they will not do their best job with the campers. Arrange for breaks during the day, especially if the weather is hot.

Staff who feel valued and have avenues for expressing ideas and concerns are more likely to return. Consider hosting a party now and then to recognize their contribution and help them find time to socialize with each other.

"We place a lot of effort into keeping our trained staff. That saves us many, many headaches. We try to figure out ways to find challenging positions for those who return; that way, they feel good about our camp and their job at it."
—DD Gass, Campfire Day Camps, Des Moines, Iowa

Training goals

The structure and content of your program will determine to a large extent how you will approach staff training. There are many training models from which to choose. Some camps carry out on-site pre-camp training the week before campers arrive. Some train during weekends, one day a week or evenings during the spring, and, if the site is available, some on-site, at other meeting places, or a combination of both. You may also want to schedule in-service training during the summer to learn new skills, improve a procedure, or help staff deal with a problem they have been having.

Volunteer staff presents other factors to consider. Volunteers may not be able, or willing, to find sufficient time to attend training sessions *and* fulfill camp responsibilities, especially when these are undertaken in the same time block. For many, weekends or evenings, especially in the spring, can be the best time for training.

Whether paid or volunteer, staff must understand that training is an *expectation of the job and participation is mandatory.* Returning staff must also attend training; after all, even the most practiced professional in any field needs periodic updates to keep current on changes in their industry and policies.

Before you undertake general staff training, you may want to consider training your administrative or leadership staff. This will enable you to draw on them later for their assistance during your general staff training.

Helpful as you start to plan your training is a review of adult education, and the various training styles and methods connected with it. Let's take a look . . .

Adult Education

As you plan and conduct your staff training, remember you are training *adults*. This can be quite a different undertaking than teaching children. Adults bring to the training experience a different set of educational requirements and expectations. For instance, adults are more accustomed to learning through a variety of training styles. Some prefer to read the information; others prefer to practice and discuss techniques. Others are visual; some are more inclined to learn by listening. Information presented in bullets or steps is often better retained than complex explanations. Active participation and a variety of methods will add interest and help meet the diverse needs of the group.

People (adults and children alike) expect to be treated with dignity and respect, and want to be valued as individuals. Adults also expect their opinions to be valued and taken seriously. Also, adults find the learning experience more meaningful when they become involved in aspects of the decision-making progress.

Adult learners are self-motivated. They must feel the information is important to the job they will be doing. They enjoy new experiences and learning that are based on real problems and real tasks. They need positive feedback to ensure personal growth and continued motivation. They may need to understand why something is done differently at your camp; the experienced perspective of the adult staff member can also be a valuable asset in learning new and better ways of running your camp and program.

Adults bring a rich mix of life experience, not only to training activities, but to your program and campers as well. With the right training they can—and will—be among your camp's most valued assets.

Pre-camp training topics

The chart in Figure 5.8 illustrates some key pre-camp training topics and/or information that should be included in a staff manual per ACA standards. Use it to identify training areas and determine your specific training methods.

You've determined the areas in which you'll want to train your staff. Now think about *how* you want to carry out that training. What method will best communicate the key lessons you want your staff to learn and remember?

First, consider some proven training methods that many camps use:

- group planning,
- presentation/lecture,
- generating/sharing ideas,
- brainstorming,
- group discussion,
- group decision making.
- task group/sharing,
- role playing observation, and
- demonstration and practice.

Planning for supervision and support of your staff

Good camp supervision doesn't just happen. Neither does support for a camp staff. You must weave systems into your administrative structure that ensure these essential areas are adequately addressed. Coming up with these systems, and making sure they do what they're supposed to do each camp day, is your job. Remember, your staff wants to do a good job. All of us do; wanting to do things well is human nature. Your role is to help your staff do just that.

Pre-Camp Training Topics

Figure 5.8

Check those topics you want to include in a manual (M) and/or those you want to include in training (T). Once you have determined what you want to include in training, consider the method you think would be most effective for staff to learn the information and the amount of time you want to spend on the topic.

Topic for Staff:	M	T	Method(s) Time(s)
Administrative Areas			
Camp background, history, and development			
Philosophy and objectives of the camp or organization			
Staff relationships and organizational chart			
Personnel policies, rules, and regulations			
Records and reports that must be filled out			
Routines — arrival and departure of campers, meal time, rest hour, mail, etc.			
Maintenance of site and facilities			
Responsibilities for first aid and healthcare			
Emergency procedures (fire drills, storm procedures, care of injured, and communication plan and procedures)			
Safety procedures for reporting incidents and accidents, dealing with intruders, missing, lost or runaway, being in public, and transportation			
Counseling and Skill Areas			
Responsibilities of camp staff when supervising campers			
Camper characteristics and behavior guidelines			
System to care for special needs of campers			
Knowledge in skill areas (OLS, waterfront, crafts, etc.)			
Guidelines for child protection			
Team building, group dynamics, games			
Appropriate behavior staff/camper and staff/staff			
Familiarize supervisors on how to supervise			
Programming Areas			
How each area functions, assigned activities, free choice			
Staff responsibilities regarding program activities			
Ordering program materials			
How to plan and carry out special programs (overnight trips, field days, trips, themes)			
How to maintain program equipment			
Staff responsibility in transportation			

A good first step is designing a system for supervision. This can be done by program area, age groups, or other job functions. Camps often use an organizational chart to help their staff visualize the staff organization. Figure 5.9 is an example of several charts.

Camp Organizational Chart

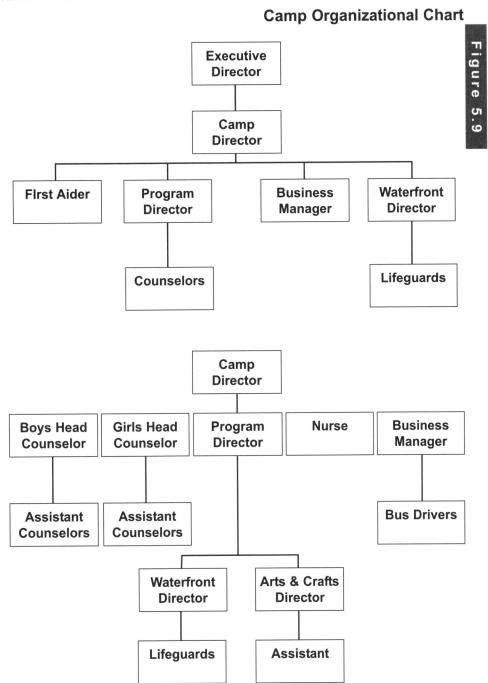

Figure 5.9

As a basic rule, supervisors should not have more than seven people under their supervision. There are five basic functions of supervisors:

- teaching staff to do their job,
- delegating responsibility,
- evaluating performance,
- improving performance, and
- dealing with problems.

A supervisor uses a variety of techniques to supervise their staff including teaching, coaching, reinforcing, modeling, and correcting. The following points may help you train supervisors and retain staff:

- Treat them as you would expect them to treat their campers (modeling).
- Provide individual opportunities for growth (teaching) and compliment them on a job well done (reinforcing). Make arrangements to listen to problems they might have.
- Understand the difference between staff who need help or practice to help them improve (coaching), and staff who create problems.
- When there are staff problems that are not solved by other methods, are safety issues, or they have purposely violated personnel policies, do not put off dealing with them (correcting). Be both consistent and fair. Focus on the behavior not the person and maintain their self-esteem.

ACA has a seven-hour supervision training available from its bookstore, *So . . . You Want to be a Supervisor!* This excellent training module will give you and your supervisors a head start on the summer.

Budget implications for your administration

As we've seen, virtually all facets of camp operation are touched by budget considerations. Camp administration is no different. In fact, probably no other area of camp operation has a more direct or immediate connection with your bottom line as the efficiency your camp administration brings to your camp. This being the case, looking closely at the budget implications of your administrative program is one of the best and most effective ways to realize significant cost savings in your camp's operation. For instance, as you look to work more efficiently, ask: "Are there ways to save administrative staff time for the more important program implementation and parent interactions?"

Your camp administrative structure will play a critical role in the success of your program. It is an essential requirement to your camp's ability to operate efficiently and cost-effectively, and deliver a superior program.

A great program deserves a solid and effective camp administration to sustain it. Give your program every advantage; work to give it the best administration you can.

Courtesy of Mark Tantrum, San Jose, California

Chapter 6

The "Big M"—Marketing and What It Can Do for You

For those of us who have passionately dedicated our careers to changing lives through the camp experience, the term marketing often carries unsavory, even negative, connotations.

In some ways this is understandable. As our culture seems to grow evermore rampantly materialistic with every passing year, perplexity can touch us who've built our professions around non-commercial priorities: child development, caring, and service. As we read about the astronomical corporate marketing budgets that perpetuate this excess of materialism, we can hardly help but question the justice of a world in which an inner-city day camp is hard-pressed to buy even basic supplies.

Marketing, of course, is not some kind of "evil empire." Marketing, in fact, can be your strongest ally in bringing about and sustaining a quality program. It also can be a prime contributor to your camp's overall mission.

Think of your marketing as an extension of your camp's educational goals. Regrettably, there are many families who are completely unfamiliar with the camp experience and what it can do developmentally for their children. If one child goes to camp because your marketing message successfully influences one of these families, you've achieved a success as important as anything you'll ever accomplish in camp.

For these and many other reasons, marketing must be front and center in your camp's operation.

Let your camp's light shine . . .

Marketing plays a role in virtually everything we do. Whether we're aware of it or not, we use marketing's techniques of persuasion in all kinds of settings: when we apply for a job, even when we court those we wish to marry. Marketing also is basic to our political process; after all, what is a lobbyist if not a marketer for a special interest? If money makes the world go 'round, marketing keeps it turning.

Let's face it: on its most basic level marketing is little more than self-promotion. Effective marketing involves singing your own praises, and doing it well enough so that people will want to listen, if not eventually join your choir themselves.

But, marketing savvy may not come as second nature to camp directors. Camp professionals, typically modest even self-effacing sorts that we are, tend to find our glory not in demonstrative self-promotion but in quiet, often unseen acts, such as helping a child in learning a new skill. Because of that, sometimes promotion may not be a thing we do well.

Well, we have to change that. The sooner you overcome any discomfort you may have about the self-promotion of your camp the better. In the camp industry, as in the hotly competitive world of business overall, *there is no room for modesty* about the good things we're trying to do.

Camp marketing consultant Steve Cony underscores how the failure to put yourself forward can limit your program.

"Modesty has no place in marketing. Your brochures, Web sites, video, direct mail, etc., are the vehicles that allow you to speak enthusiastically about all that you do for campers. You cannot expect people to first admire your honesty, then take over and build your sales message for you—in their own heads, all by themselves. You have to tell them what you do, then tell them again, and tell them a third time." [1]

Marketing your camp is an all-year activity. You can't wait until two weeks before camp season to start getting the word out about your program. Never miss an opportunity throughout the year to plan and incorporate into your camp's operational structure the kind of creative and well-focused marketing that brings results.

Or to put it another way: no factor can limit the success of your marketing more than your reluctance to tell your camp's story, and tell it well. Modesty can lead to marketing failures that can, in short order, lead to the complete failure of your camp. So, when it comes to telling the world about the great things your camp does, sing out loud and clear! It's like the old camp song says: don't hide your light under a bushel; you gotta let it shine.

Developing your marketing plan

Where do you start? Well, as they say, before you can *do* you have to *plan,* so let's begin with your marketing plan.

Your marketing plan enables you to identify your key marketing messages—those features or attributes of your camp that your research (or instinct!) suggests will be the strongest selling point with the target audience you're going after. It also maps the course of action you'll need to take to reach your potential customers with your key messages, or selling points.

In addition, your marketing plan should outline specific tactics (for example, brochures, Web site, videos, or direct mail pieces) that will get the word out about your camp. Your plan also should contain a timeline for program execution. Generally speaking, a camp marketing plan covers everything relating to promotion: advertising, public relations, direct mail, and external (that is, customer-targeted) communications.

Your work in Chapters 1 and 2 should have helped you gather and analyze much of the information you'll need to get your plan started: the demographics of your potential customers, assessments of competing camps, and so on.

Remember, the development of your marketing plan should be a team effort whenever possible, involving members of your camp committee, staff, and other appropriate camp partners. One more thing: don't forget the "O" word. *Make sure your marketing goals are consistent with your outcomes.*

Now let's get started putting your plan together.

Finding your key marketing messages

One of your first orders of business in drafting your marketing plan is to identify your marketing message. Think back on the research you've already done and ask yourself, "What is the key selling point of our camp?" At this point, you need to take a hard and honest look at whatever it is that makes your camp special, for instance specific program or staffing-related strengths, location . . . really, anything at all that sets your camp apart, or is a major selling point.

The important word here is *honesty*. Steve Cony puts it this way: "You must do some soul-searching, some group discussions involving senior staff, and perhaps even some organized research among your customers—all to determine what exactly makes your camp different and unique. You must not be lulled into believing that those photos of your waterfront are magical, even though you maintain the docks and fleet meticulously." [2]

© Girl Scouts of Limberlost Council, 2002/Bryce Hunt

"It's all in the numbers . . ."

Your research into your target market and demographics is key to a successful marketing plan. In addition to the available Web-based resources discussed in Chapter 2, information from sources close at hand, for instance, demographic data your camp has collected in previous seasons, can be helpful. Registration information, parent and camper evaluations and surveys, and input from returning staff are all excellent sources of information. Use it to update and maintain your camp database. Your database should include, at a minimum, key information such as camper ages, genders, income levels, addresses, and ethnic identity.

Camper and parent evaluations are some of the best research tools available to the camp director for an established camp. Chances are that much of what you need to know about your campers can be found right in your files in a folder marked "evaluations."

Evaluations give you an inside look into what program and other elements were important to parents and to the camper . . . the positive *and* negative.

If your camp is new and you don't have information from past years to work from, start collecting it now. Begin building your database by drawing on the information you uncovered about your demographics in Chapter 2. Some questions can spark new insights into how you want to market your camp:

- What percentage of your past campers have returned to your camp?
- Do you want to recruit more first-time campers?
- Do you want to recruit more campers from varying economic levels or different cultures?
- Who else is providing a summer experience to your prospective campers?

Remember, in most cases, a child in the fourth grade or higher makes the decision to attend camp. For this reason, your marking information should speak to them first. After you reach your camper, parents will then want the details. For younger children, the parent will choose the camp and make the final decision. So target your message to them.

Know the answer to parents' questions before they're asked . . .

Know what kinds of questions parents want to know when choosing a camp. ACA's Web site has a list of questions parents should ask directors. As a director you should be ready to answer these questions. A review of the information below can help.

How to Choose a Camp — With more than 12,000 camps in the United States, choosing one may seem overwhelming. However, selecting the right program often boils down to knowing your options and asking the right questions. The American Camping Association (ACA) offers the following guidelines when choosing a camp to help ensure that it is an experience your child will cherish for a lifetime.

Ask the Right Questions — Below are some important questions to ask the camp director, as well as the answers you want to hear:

- **What is the educational and career background of the camp director?** — The camp director should possess a bachelor's degree, have completed in-service training within the past three years and have at least sixteen weeks of camp administrative experience.
- **What is the camper return rate?** — While every camp is clearly not right for every person, a large number of returning campers usually indicates a high level of satisfaction with the camp's programming and operation.
- **How old are the counselors? What percentage are return counselors from past years? What qualities, certification and experience does the director look for in staff?** — Among the counseling/ program staff, 80 percent or more should be 18 years or older. Any counselor under 18 must be at least two years older than the camper they are supervising. Some staff turnover is natural, but most camps have between 40 and 60 percent of staff return each year. If the rate is lower, find out why.
- **What is the ratio of counselors to campers?** — The ratio should be based on the ages of the campers and their special needs. Severely mentally-disabled campers require a ratio of one staff to one camper. Non-disabled resident campers require one staff for every six campers ages six to eight, one staff for every eight campers ages nine to fourteen, and one staff for every ten campers ages fifteen to eighteen. Day campers require one staff for every eight campers ages six to eight, one staff for every ten campers ages nine to fourteen, and one staff for every twelve campers ages fifteen to eighteen.
- **What is the camp's program philosophy?** — Some promote competition and healthy rivalry among camp teams, while others encourage cooperative learning. Knowing your child's personality and learning style will help you select a camp with the appropriate philosophy.
- **What are the safety and medical accommodations at the camp?** — If your child has special needs, are programs, accommodations, and facilities adequate?

- **What is the transportation system?** — Find out what type of vehicles are used (typically it's vans or buses) and how often they are inspected by qualified mechanics.
- **Ask the director to describe the camp's driver training and on-going safety awareness programs.**
- **Ask if it will be possible to visit the camp before enrolling your child.**
- **Ask for names of camper families to contact for their impressions of the camp.**
- **Is the camp accredited by the American Camping Association?** — ACA accreditation verifies that a camp has complied with up to three hundred standards for health, safety, and program quality which are recognized by courts of law and government regulators. At least once every three years, an outside team of trained camp professionals observe the camp in session to verify compliance. If a camp you are considering is not ACA-accredited, it is important to find out why.

© *Girl Scouts of Limberlost Council, 2002/Bryce Hunt*

Identifying and documenting your key marketing messages

If your research reveals that your camp holds a unique or strong competitive edge, you'll want to make sure that's reflected in your key marketing messages.

Figure 6.1 illustrates a chart that can help you simplify the task of identifying and documenting your key marketing messages. The list includes many examples of key marketing messages. To use the chart, begin with your outcomes then tie them back to those program characteristics that make your camp program special, and would make good marketing messages. Add others that are unique to your camp.

Key Marketing Messages

Figure 6.1

Begin with your outcomes.
What are you promising parents?
How will their child be different as a result of the day camp experience?
What are your program characteristics?

- A group of campers who return annually
- A staff of which at least half return annually
- Gives parents an opportunity to talk to staff
- Gives parents an opportunity to talk to current campers/parents
- Provides campers with an opportunity to choose some of their activities
- Maintains staff/camper ratios of 1:6 for children under 12 and 1:8 for children over 12
- Offers an environment where children are under constant supervision
- Offers non-competitive programs
- Offers competitive programs
- Offers parents good value for their money
- Offers a variety of program activities
- Builds skills through special programs including . . .
- Has an impeccable safety record
- Offers opportunity to gain skills in social interaction
- Offers convenient, safe transportation
- Offers an extended-day program for the convenience of working parents
- Offers a program with age-appropriate activities
- Screens and trains a qualified staff
- Meets the needs of children with disabilities

- Offers a coed program . . . or offers a single-sex program
- Provides healthy lunches . . . cookouts . . . snacks . . . beverages
- Provides health services
- Provides a unique outdoor setting
- Offers fun adventures by day and allows campers to return home to familiar environment at night
- Is accredited by the American Camping Association

Next rank the messages according to importance. Be sure that your outcomes and the most important five or six key marketing messages are communicated at every opportunity.

Marketing to your target population

You have your target population squarely in your marketing sights. Now before you pull the trigger, you'll need to assemble your marketing tool kit, the portfolio of promotional tools you'll use to tell the world about your camp. These tools, which comprise the tactical elements of your marketing plan, can include brochures, videos/DVDs, camper testimonial sheets, Web sites, newsletters, posters, camp fact sheets, Frequently Asked Questions, direct mail pieces, and public relations activities. In fact, it can be just about anything that effectively communicates your marketing messages.

The tools you use to publicize your camp can be as simple or elaborate as you like (and your budget will allow). But whether simple, fancy, or something in between—the important criteria your publicity tools must reflect include:

✓ projecting a professional image for your camp,
✓ accuracy and truthfulness, and
✓ clearly and directly delivering your key marketing messages in a way that's consistent with overall marketing objectives.

Brochures, for example, need not be costly or slick, but they *must* clearly reflect your message. This is true for all your tools.

What are some commonly used promotional tools? Let's take a look.

Printed Materials

Brochures, fliers, newsletters, direct mail (personal letters) and letterhead, business cards, posters, etc.

Printed materials are probably the most commonly used tactic, one that's ideally suited to reaching your targeted audiences. They can be distributed through a variety of methods that include the mail, schools, businesses, and display booths, to name a few.

Brochures/Fliers — Information that parents expect a brochure or flyer to include:

- program activities offered,
- information about staff and staff–child ratios,
- number of sessions and dates,
- contact information,
- location,
- snack/food-related information,
- safety-related information (such as number of staff trained in first aid/CPR),
- whether your camp is ACA accredited,
- professional affiliations,
- the benefits of day camp experience, and
- refund policies.

Direct Mail — Personal letters from the director and/or other staff and campers are an effective tactic for camp promotion. They are personal and can be very cost-effective; most important, direct mail pieces can be precisely targeted. A direct mail letter can include new programs you're offering, introduction to new staff members, updates on new equipment, and other information. To accurately target your direct mail piece, you'll need a mailing list. This can originate from your own database of campers. You can also purchase a list. Purchased lists, however, can greatly add to your promotional expenses.

Newsletters — These offer a very effective way to reach parents and campers during the off-season and communicate updates or new information.

Other Printed Materials — You also can create other print pieces that get the word out about your camp, for instance disposable materials such as paper placemats for use in local restaurants, and grocery store bags, signs with tear-off phone numbers, etc.

Make sure your printed materials have a consistent image and a uniform look, and reflect your key marketing messages. Put your logo on everything you can. Remember, it is essential that you communicate a clear and concise message about who you are and what you are doing.

Photographs offer a visually appealing way to brighten up your printed materials. Choose photos that tell the story of your day camp. (It is best to have close-up pictures with five or fewer people in the photograph.) Show competent staff members and activities that are safe. Make sure kids are shown in appropriate safety gear. And don't forget the photo captions; because captions are almost always read, make them tell your story as well. (If you do not have good pictures or photo permissions you may need to use art and graphics to tell your story.)

Print materials such as brochures, posters, and other recruitment items may need to be coordinated with your printing company. Don't forget lead time with printed pieces; they may take several months to complete, so begin developing yours as early as possible.

The Media

You can draw on the considerable promotion power of print and electronic media to get the word out about your day camp. The media is always looking for good child-related stories, including those about camp, especially as camp season approaches.

Print Media

Newspaper Articles (don't forget community and suburban) — It helps to establish a relationship with those who would be writing or reporting your stories prior to the camping season. Put reporters who cover the "camp beat" on your newsletter mailing list.

Electronic Media — Radio and television often will run Public Service Announcements (PSAs) for free if your organization is not-for-profit: take advantage of this great promotional tool. Local talk shows also can provide good opportunities to promote your camp. Remember, broadcast media typically requires a minimum of four weeks lead time between the time you pitch a story idea and when it actually airs.

Press Releases — Your press releases should be no more than one page long, and should lead with two to three sentences that have solid news content. Good topics include: interesting people at your camp, a unique camper, a unique program you offer, an invitation to an open house, or an event prior to camp. Make sure to follow-up with the press release by a phone call to confirm receipt.

"To keep our camp front-and-center in the public eye, I get out as much as I can in the community. For instance, Public Access TV was recently doing a show on summer camps, and they wanted some representation from local camps. I know they do these every year, so I always call before camp season and tell them, 'If you need anything, let me know.' I also make sure I let the local papers know I'm the 'camp expert' they should call if they need a quote for a story. Because, you know, if you're in camping, you are an expert."
—Chris Winkler, YMCA Camp Eagle Rock, Charlotte, North Carolina

Internet

Set up a Web site about your day camp or include information about camp on your organization's Web site. Remember to include an FAQ section addressing parents' concerns (i.e., "Who," "What," "When," "Where," and "How"). Be sure to answer e-mail promptly. These statistics illustrate how effective a communication medium the Internet has become. According to the U.S. Census Bureau, September 2001:

- 51 percent of U.S. households had one or more computers in 2000.
- 80 percent of these households had at least one member using the Internet.
- 25 percent of U.S. residents use the Web to search for information.
- 88 percent of adults and 73 percent of children who are online at home use e-mail.
- Among family households with incomes below $25,000, nearly 30 percent had a computer and about 20 percent had Internet access.
- About 77 percent of white non-Hispanic and 72 percent of Asian and Pacific Islander children lived in households with computers, while only 43 percent of African American children and 37 percent of Hispanic children did.

Other Promotional Strategies

These would include displays, promotional items, community events, collaborations, word-of-mouth.

Promotional Items — You can put your logo on anything that can be printed on. Key chains, pens, shirts, calendars, watches, flying discs, squeegee balls, cups, hats, etc.

Collaborations — Partner with another camp or organization to cut promotional costs. Shared brochures, flyers, etc.

Displays — Malls, bulletin boards, and posters can be created inexpensively. Displaying posters in business windows, lobbies, churches, schools, laundromats, doctor's offices and shopping areas are effective at getting parents'/campers' attention. Don't forget to include a phone number e-mail address, and contact name for more information.

Outdoor Advertising — Billboards may be leased or possibly paid for through local business owners.

Community Events — Open House, reunions, off-season camping events, display at fairs or carnivals.

Word of Mouth — Talk about day camp. Parent Teacher Associations, service clubs, city leagues or sport/recreation leagues, youth clubs, faith-based youth groups, neighborhood associations and other organizational events. Staff, campers and their parents are your best promoters. Give them a good, safe program to talk about.

No matter what promotional tools you choose to use, keep one thing in mind: You must accurately target for marketing efforts to your customers—that is, your campers and their parents. In developing your tools' messages, you have to think like your audience, and communicate in terms they can understand. You must also consider where your target audience will be most likely to see your message. For instance, since 72 percent of Asian or Pacific Islander children live in a household with a computer, Internet marketing to that target group could be very successful. Consider alternatives to reach your audience: schools, stores, local newspapers, doctor/dentist offices, churches, and neighborhood centers. It also helps to fold a strong "customer-benefits focus" into the message: clearly tell what benefit your camp can bring to the child who attends.

Great publicity . . . cheap!

As long as we're talking about cost, let's clear up one popular misconception: money does not have to be a limiting factor in your marketing efforts.

The word marketing often conjures up images of big, splashy "whoop-de-dos," ones that are usually heavier on so-called style than substance. Actually, marketing—if it's undertaken creatively—can deliver surprising results for comparatively little money. This is good news for camps that do not have the resources to develop lavish brochures or videos, elaborate Web sites, and other high-cost marketing pieces.

Many books are available that can give you additional tactics for low-cost "guerrilla" marketing, PR, and promotion strategies. These will prove to be an invaluable resource for the camp director who is high on ideas and energy, but low on funds.

PR: the low-cost, high-performance marketing tool

As an affordable and effective publicity technique, public relations is hard to beat. With PR there are no brochures to print, ads to buy, or expensive videos to produce. In fact, if you have a practiced in-house writer who likes to wear the PR hat, your PR-related publicity can be had for the cost of that person's salary. We've covered some basic PR tactics earlier. Now, let's look at how PR is working for Mary's Camp ARTastic.

Sue, a single mother of two eight-year-old boys, opens the Sunday newspaper and reads about a new camp in the area that offers a unique art program, one that helps children explore creative expression and learn to work well with others. Interested in learning more, she picks up the phone and calls the camp director who is mentioned in the article. The next day she visits the camp, takes a tour and ends her stay by registering her boys for the upcoming session. (By the way, the woman's call was one of *two dozen* just like it the camp received as a result of the article.)

It didn't end there. The next year the boys wanted two of their friends to go with them. Positive recommendations from previous campers or their parents are the kind of word-of-mouth referrals that are the best marketing tool a camp can have.

This scenario shows how effective the "unseen hand" of public relations can be. It all started with the director writing a brief press release that clearly and compellingly described this unique new camp program. Mary e-mailed it to the city editor of the local paper, and by the end of the day got a call from a reporter requesting a site visit, interview and photos.

If the camp had to pay for the coverage they got in the three-column story (in a paper with a circulation of 425,000) it would have cost thousands. As it was, the cost of this windfall of publicity was zero.

Public relations is a low-cost, effective way to get your camp's name out in front of your prospective customers. Public relations uses the news interest of an event, such as our example of a director's new sport program, to gain publicity in newspapers or other media. PR is especially effective because the coverage it creates suggests an independent third-party endorsement by the media. The people who won't look twice at an ad will eagerly read an interesting news account. That's why even the most expensive ad won't buy you the kind of publicity PR can bring you.

Of course, there is always the possibility that your event will not qualify as news on a given day, especially a busy news day. But more often than not, PR can be an effective way to get your camp's name in front of the public and potential customers.

There are many other resources that can tell you how to plan and run effective PR programs. But to get you going, here are a couple of staple PR tactics that will be useful to the new camp director:

- ✓ **Press releases** — Hook editors by offering *newsworthy* information about your camp. Remember, if what you send is *not* newsworthy, then find a way to *make it newsworthy*. Otherwise it'll go straight to the circular file.
- ✓ **Camp backgrounder** — These one- or two-page pieces, which are sometimes included in press kits, provide background on your camp and program.
- ✓ **Media tours** — These tours can do much to familiarize your local media with your program and the general value camps bring to the support of youth development. If a single photograph is worth a thousand words, just think how much publicity you would get out of a three-minute live broadcast about your camp's opening day.

PR offers virtually limitless opportunities to publicize your camp. As with any promotional effort, the ingenuity, creativity, and persistence you bring to your PR efforts will pay off in the kind of high-profile media hits that can drive substantial interest in your camp and bring in customers.

Bringing it all together: your marketing strategy chart

Developing a marketing strategy chart is an excellent way to identify and document the "Who," "Where," "How," and "Estimated Cost" of your marketing campaign. Figure 6.2 shows a sample of Camp ARTastic's strategy. (A blank one is on your CD.)

Here's how you can put it to work for you:

- In the first column list groups that you want to target.
- In column two list entities at, or through which, this target group receives its information.
- In column three list the techniques you will need to be the most effective in promoting your camp (your "hows").
- In column four list the projected cost of the activity.

After the form is completed, weigh the costs against your available budget, prioritize the list of promotional techniques, or look for ways to get donations or reduce costs.

No matter how creative or low-cost your marketing program may be, chances are it will almost certainly tap your overall budget. You may want to track the strategies that were the most effective to help with your plans for next year. For example, flyers can be distributed in different colors so that the return "tear off" will indicate where it was distributed. Perhaps an easier way is to ask on the registration information, in phone inquiries, or evaluations where they heard about camp.

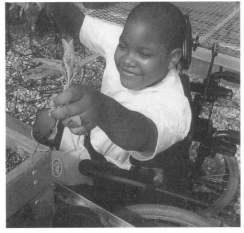

Courtesy of Kamp A-Kom-Plish,
Nanjemoy, Maryland

Marketing Strategy Chart

Figure 6.2

✓ Who – Describe your target population
✓ Where – Places and sources that reach the target population
✓ How – Most effective promotional technique for this group
✓ Estimated Cost

Who	Where	How	Estimated Cost
Parents of 6-to-8-year-olds	Organization Web site, Internet camp listings	Information on outcomes and addressing FAQ	Still compiling
Local children and grandchildren of local retirees	Children's Art Festival	Set up a booth with information about what our camp has to offer, and raffle tickets for a free week at day camp

Have a simple craft that attending children can make

Campership information | $300 booth fee |
ZIP codes: 46338, 44214 46487	*City News Gazette*	Ad in the summer camp edition	$1000
Returning campers	Web site	Quarterly newsletter and pictures on Web site	$0
	Direct mail	Brochure with pictures of last summer	$3000
Private and public school families in the area — ages 6 to 8	Direct mail	Flyer with Web site address and number for requesting brochure	$550
Culturally-diverse youth	Community Cultural Center

Ethnic media | Flyers and posters, parents meeting, campership info, weekly newsletter, radio spots in Spanish | $50

Free PSA |
| Elementary age youth | Local schools, toy stores, children's clothing stores, pediatric offices, library, etc. | Flyers, posters | $300 |

Courtesy of Echo Lake Southwoods, Paradox, New York

Printing

An understanding of basic printing will help minimize costs when you're producing brochures and other printed marketing materials for your camp. Here are some things to keep in mind:

- For commercial color printing it is best to work with someone experienced in that business. For marketing materials printing black or one color only, consider working with a student who may be eager for the chance to add to his or her résumé.
- When hiring a graphic designer, make sure he or she includes "preparing all files for printing" as part of the services. You should be given a CD with all files, fonts, and graphics used in the piece. This way you will have the files to adapt for use in future marketing materials.
- Many commercial printers have in-house graphic designers and can bid on the design portion of your marketing materials as well as the actual printing. Ask the printer to provide two quotes, one including graphic design and one with printing alone.
- When you obtain costs on printing, ask for an alternative price using recycled paper and/or soy-based inks. It may be more economical and will also demonstrate that your camp is concerned about the environment.
- Confirm with the printer the terms of their quote and make sure it includes all possible costs for your project, including any revisions, overruns, and shipping.
- Investigate the pros and cons of bulk-rate mailings. Information can be found on the U.S. Postal Service Web site: www.usps.gov (keyword: bulk rate).
- Consider USPS rules if you plan to include advertising in mailed marketing materials. There are rules about whether you can have a sponsor advertise in not-for-profit bulk mailings. In most cases they can be recognized for donations but not advertise. Check with your post office.
- Know when to use envelopes or a self-mailer. A self-mailer of one page may be too light to go through a postage machine or survive the mailing process. In addition, know how to prepare the mailing (hand addressing, labels, or database computer list; also use the entire ZIP code + 4 in the address). The USPS offers the services of a "Mailpiece Design Analyst." Contact information is available at www.usps.gov.
- Obtain bids from a direct mail service and compare cost and time factors with assembling the mailing in-house with staff or volunteers.

If a tree falls . . .

To refashion a bit of philosophy, "If a tree falls in your camp's back 40 during off-season will anyone hear it?" Probably not.

If your camp offers the best program going; has the most innovative, popular activities, and the best-qualified staff, *and no one hears or knows about it,* will you be in business past your first season? If you are, it will be one of those little wondrous occurrences that make for great stories around the campfire.

Promotion of your camp is essential. Don't make the mistake of focusing on the development of your program and administration to the exclusion of your marketing. Your program, staff, and camp successes will give you a great story to tell. Be sure to tell it. *The louder the better.*

[Notes]

1 Steve Cony, "Camp Un-Traditions," *Camping* March/April 2003 p 46

2 Steve Cony, "Find Your Niche!," *Camping* Jan./Feb 2003 p 14

Courtesy of Camp Greystone, Tuxedo, North Carolina

Chapter 7

Keeping Your Campers Safe . . . and Your Camp Protected— Risk Management and Crisis Communication

It's a day camp director's worst nightmare. Your pager goes off; you return the call. You hear the rapid-fire, panicked voice of one of your counselors tell you that one of your kids—a boy—has been hit by lightning. The cloudburst came unexpectedly, he's explaining tearfully . . . "We were doing our best to clear the kids off the field, but . . ."

Tragedies such as this find their way into the headlines all the time. But what if one should hit your camp? Are you and your team ready? What about your risk management and crisis communications plans: are they living, up-to-date documents that you can activate at a moment's notice, or simply some pages you put together as a formality that, you think, are in the bottom drawer of the green file cabinet?

Are you and your staff prepared to handle the seventy-five to one hundred media calls per day that are likely to start coming in by lunch? Are you ready to face a TV camera, taking fast-ball questions from a bulldog reporter demanding to know "*how* a day camp could possibly be so remiss as to let kids play on a soccer field during an electrical storm?"

Maybe it's just human nature that causes many of us take the view that "bad things aren't going to happen to me/us/my camp." This perspective is as short-sighted as it is dead wrong. Ask anyone who has been through a significant unexpected event. Bad things *do* happen. And they *can* happen to you.

You'll never be able to completely eliminate risk from your camp. But to meet it effectively, it is *imperative* that you have in place the procedures that will enable you to competently and calmly manage any situation that arises.

Good risk management and crisis communications preparation can save your camp's reputation, protect it from potentially devastating legal action, and ensure maximum safety for your campers, staff and volunteers. It also can give you the peace of mind to know that if something *does* happen, you'll be adequately prepared to deal with it professionally and effectively.

What is risk management?

Risk management is everything you do to protect your operation, including how you handle any crisis that might arise. Good risk management begins with a risk management plan that outlines a structured process for protecting your camp's assets, especially its human assets, from injury or loss.

A good risk management plan safeguards not only participants and staff, but also protects your officers, directors, staff, and volunteers. In addition, your risk management plan outlines a strategy for continued operation should an incident occur in your camp.

Understanding risk management

Risk management plans are systems to identify, evaluate, reduce, prevent, or control the loss of resources—both tangible and intangible assets. Tangible assets include money, property, equipment. Among your intangible assets are your reputation, future business, and so on.

Knowing what your assets are worth is important. Tangible assets are easier than intangible ones to place a value on; for instance, it is difficult to place a value on your reputation.

Consider placing your exposure to risk into three categories. This will make it easier for you to identify, analyze, and plan for protection of your assets.

- **Human** — These exposures dictate the standard of care you must provide; they also identify your human resources, e.g., talented staff or volunteers.
- **Financial** — These exposures involve financial operations or contracts you enter into.
- **Property** — Exposures that involve your physical property, that is buildings, equipment, or other "hard" assets.

Once you have identified your exposures, consider the best methods to evaluate, reduce, prevent, or control the loss of resources and avoid, transfer, retain, or reduce the exposure. In some cases you can use more than one method; however, you must analyze each exposure and determine the best method or methods to prevent loss.

To avoid a risk, you may wish to simply eliminate an activity. For example, hang-gliding may be too risky to consider; or perhaps transporting children in fifteen-passenger vans is too much of a risk.

You may also opt to transfer risk. This is commonly done by purchasing insurance or paying someone else to assume the risk through a contract. For example, liability insurance can protect you from assuming all the loss should legal action be taken against you. Or you contract with a bus company to handle your transportation instead of purchasing buses and providing this service yourself.

Waivers, hold-harmless, and release statements that campers or parents sign can transfer or waive responsibility for certain actions to the participant or a sponsoring group. However, in most states a parent cannot sign away the rights of a child to hold the camp accountable once they become an adult. For this reason, a camp should consult their attorney for wording and/or use of hold-harmless agreements.

Your level of risk may become acceptable when you decide you can afford to pay for any loss that may occur as a result of it; for example, loss of program equipment that may normally happen each summer. Another situation where risk may be acceptable is when you retain part of the loss by a deductible on an insurance policy.

When it comes to lessening your overall risk, the best method is reduction of your risk. Regardless of what else you decide to do you will probably want to take measures to reduce the possibility of loss. Ways to decrease risk include hiring and training qualified staff, having age-appropriate equipment, maintaining operational procedures for each activity, and so on.

It's important to note that all the planning and prevention strategies in the world cannot prevent an accident or crisis. For this reason, a key part of your risk management-related planning must be crisis management; that is, what you do when a crisis does occur. Good crisis management, by definition, means possible loss reduction and related risks. Basic to this planning is establishing emergency procedures, putting in place a crisis communication plan, having on-site qualified people to provide first aid, and other related safeguards.

Courtesy of Camp Aldersgate, Inc., Little Rock, Arkansas/Matt Bradley

A closer look at a risk management plan

A fully developed risk management plan is actually a collection of many smaller detailed plans; for instance, a health-care plan, insurance plan, crisis management plan, and so on. An overview of a risk management plan can be found in a chart developed by ACA. The chart in Figure 7.1 shows examples that will give you ideas about reducing, preventing, or controlling your potential losses.

As you see, the chart shows three major categories of risk exposure:

- Human Exposures or Liabilities (including Standard of Care Liabilities and Loss to Human Resources),
- Financial Exposures or Liabilities (including Operational Financial Liabilities and Contract Liabilities), and
- Property Exposures or Liabilities.

The first step in managing your exposures is to identify them. As you develop your chart, place a check by those exposures applicable to your day camp. Then, determine how best to handle the risk. The chart shows examples of damage or loss, sample techniques to reduce, prevent or control loss, and it provides a way for you to think through your best method to handle the exposure.

The chart also reflects ACA standards. Whether your camp is accredited or not, the ACA standards represent the standards of the industry. For this reason, should any legal action arise as a result of an incident at your camp, ACA standards will probably be used as best practices to evaluate your camp in court. As you are planning, it is helpful for you to know what those practices are.

Once you have decided on how you will handle your exposures, you must begin writing your plan. This can be challenging. It may help to rank the areas; in this way you can begin with the most important potential risk, or assemble a team to take care of different areas. Each year you may only have to review the plan and make minor updates.

Figure 7.1

Risk Exposure Chart (referenced by ACA Standards)

Check all that apply to your camp			
Standard of Care Liabilities (tort or third-party liabilities)	**Examples or Type of Illness/ Injury or Damage Caused by:**	**Sample Techniques to Reduce, Prevent or Control Loss**	**Identify Risk Control Methods and Technique(s) and Steps Taken**
❏ General Duty of Care	Damage to others caused by negligence. (Many are described in specific areas below.)	Good general liability insurance in addition to any exclusions or additional coverage described below. Umbrella liability insurance for catastrophic accidents. OM-11	
❏ Directors and Officers	Decisions made by directors, boards, committees or lack of policies or procedures	Informed decision makers establish policies consistent with common practice or standards of the field, D & O insurance	
❏ Property of Others	Equipment not owned by the camp	Regulations for possession and use OM-12, TR-13	
❏ Employer/Employee Relationship -harassment -slander -discrimination	Inappropriate actions, including criminal behavior, by employer or other staff wrongful dismissal, invasion of privacy, discrimination based on age, race, religion, sex or disability, etc.	Staff hiring policies, personnel policies, training process, policy on search and seizure, Bona Fide Occupational Qualification, sexual abuse liability insurance, employment practices liability insurance (BFOQ), etc. HR-3,5,8	
❏ Food Service	Unsafe water, hazardous foods containing infectious or toxic microorganisms; e.g., e-coli, salmonella, etc.	Procedures for storage and handling potentially hazardous foods and sanitation, controlled access, etc. SF-5,22,23,26-32, PD-*1	
❏ Environmental Impairment and Pollution	Sewage, toxic materials, leaks of underground tanks, insect/weed control, use of chemicals, etc.	Garbage storage capacity, leakproof, environmental impact plan, etc. SF*2, 24,25, PD-*1,3	
❏ Maintenance	Broken equipment, bunk bed rails, rotted stairs, unsafe electrical or gas lines, shower water temperatures, vehicle mechanical failure, damaged program equipment, etc.	Workers' compensation insurance, maintenance plan, identified cutoff points, trained personnel, emergency exits, annual fire equipment and electrical evaluation, etc. SF-*1,3,4,6,7,20, TR-15,16,PC-11,-A-28, PT-14, PH-13	

Human Exposures or Liabilities:

	Examples or Type of Illness/ Injury or Damage Caused by:	Sample Techniques to Reduce, Prevent or Control Loss	Identify Risk Control Methods and Technique(s) and Steps Taken
☐ Attractive Nuisances	Failure to control access or unauthorized use of ropes course, lake, pool, firearms, etc.	Fences, signs, security system, etc. OM-*1,7, PD-15,PC-8,10, PA-11,12,13, PH-7	
Standard of Care Liabilities (tort or third-party liabilities)			
☐ Staff Selection/Training (volunteer or paid)	Lack of screening or training, unqualified staff, etc. Violation of child labor laws and discrimination laws.	Driver training, training for late hires, in-service training, work permits and proof of age procedures, knowledge of laws. OM-14, TR-9,18,19, HR-3,10,17, PD-*1, HW-12	
☐ Staff Supervision/Behavior (volunteer or paid)	Failure to supervise staff; drunkenness or drug use by staff, etc.	Supervision training, guidelines for appropriate and inappropriate behavior. HR-18-21	
☐ Participant Supervision	Failure to supervise adequately, not maintaining appropriate camper-to-staff ratio, camper-to-camper child abuse, release of camper to unauthorized person, etc.	Procedures for transporting persons, procedures for prevention of child abuse, appropriate camper behavior techniques, regular analysis of incidents, required documentation, etc. Child abduction liability insurance. OM-5-10,12,15-19, TR-4-11,18, HR-9,10,14,PD-*1,11,24, PT-16	
☐ Health Services	Failure to provide appropriate first aid or emergency care; failure to meet special medical needs or dispense medications properly; exposure to bloodborne pathogens, bioterrorism, diseases carried by insects or animals, etc.	Health-care plan, qualified health-care staff, user group information, etc. Exposure Control Plan (OSHA). SF-14-21, HW-*1-23, OM-3,5,6,13, PD-10,TR-12, PA-7, PT-*1, PH-10	
☐ Program Activities	Inadequate safety regulations and emergency procedures; failure to provide qualified leadership, inform parents of risk, etc.	Safe and appropriate equipment, signed permissions for participation, supplementary insurance, certifications, etc. All specialized activity standards. OM-*7,8-21, TR-7,8,11,12, PD-4,5,8,10,12-24, HW-13,14,22	
☐ Personal Injury From -abuse -assault -invasion of privacy -discrimination	Inappropriate actions, including criminal behavior, by staff or other campers; lack of protection in public places or from intruders; camper or staff recruitment practices; misuse of	Written safety regulations, personnel policies, implementation of ADA requirements and privacy rule, guidelines for release of personal information etc. Criminal records.	

continued on next page...

Figure 7.1

Standard of Care Liabilities (tort or third-party liabilities)	Examples or Type of Illness/ Injury or Damage Caused by:	Sample Techniques to Reduce, Prevent or Control Loss	Identify Risk Control Methods and Technique(s) and Steps Taken
❑ Defective or Tampered Products	Contaminated food, defective program or safety equipment, etc.	Credible food and equipment source, controlled access, crisis management plan, etc. PD-4	
❑ False Advertising	Misleading or incomplete information on facilities, activities or personnel, etc.	Brochures, videos and written material that correctly describes facilities, staff, program, etc. PD-7	
❑ Health Care Malpractice	Inappropriate actions by health-care staff,	Knowledge of individual's malpractice insurance or coverage with supplementary or general liability insurance, licensed to practice in state where camp is located.	
❑ Vehicle Operation	Passengers exceed capacity, lack of seat belts, driver not qualified, improper loading or unloading, poor selection of commercial provider, non-compliance with regulations regarding passenger vans and CDL driver drug and alcohol testing, etc.	Insurance, safety regulations, credible vehicle provider, safety checks, maintaining safety reports, etc. OM-11, TR-*1-4, 14-19, HR-3-6, 9, PT-15	
❑ Sponsorship	Lending endorsement to an activity not in your control; the image of cosponsors.	Appropriate insurance, board review of endorsements/sponsorships.	

Loss to Human Resources (Campers, Staff and Volunteers)	Considerations or effects of human loss on:	Sample Techniques to Control, Reduce, or Prevent Loss	Identify Risk Control Methods and Technique(s) and Steps Taken
❑ Injury from accident ❑ Illness preventing participation ❑ Disability (long- or short-term) ❑ Death ❑ Disease ❑ Psychological impairment ❑ _____	• loss of income if activity cannot be offered • staffing for rental group/contracted services • public credibility • campers and staff due to stress of incidents or results of accidents • closing camp due to epidemic/ illness, terrorism	• Arrangements with crisis intervention services/psychological support • Insurance for loss of income • Legal support • PR procedures • Back-up staff • Procedures to deal with crises, appoint spokespersons, crisis communication plan • Plan for handling complaints	

Financial Exposures or Liabilities:

Check all that apply to your camp **Operational Financial Liabilities**	**Financial Damage Caused by:**	**Sample Techniques to Control, Reduce, or Prevent Loss**	**Identify Risk Control Methods and Technique(s) and Steps Taken**
☐ Petty cash ☐ Cash receipts ☐ Cash disbursements ☐ Reimbursements ☐ Authority to purchase ☐ Authority to pay ☐ Authority to enter into contracts ☐ Inventory control ☐ Bank reconciliations	Poor or no procedures/policies to prevent: • theft • embezzlement • inadequate records • financial commitments beyond budget or ability to pay • bankruptcy	• Crime insurance. • Policies/procedures that specify who has authority to control access to funds and records. Use of professional accounting services. • Policies on staff reimbursement. • External audit or review. • Regular training for persons responsible for finance. • Use of Generally Accepted Accountings Principles (GAAP). • Bonding employees handling money.	
☐ Vacation Accrual ☐ Payroll Accrual	• Allowing vacation or payroll to accrue beyond ability to pay or to replace staff in a timely manner. • Obligation or commitment to pay for time worked.	Personnel policies specifying use of vacation time; current knowledge and compliance with federal and state employment laws, etc.	
☐ Computer System	• Perils or events that affect computer system; i.e., viruses, vandalism, lightning. • Losses from electronic business transactions, security, data loss, infringement of copyright, etc.	Risk-control policies in use; anti-virus software and system firewalls; insurance, training, etc. Compliance with Children's Online Privacy Protection Act (COPPA).	
☐ Government Regulations and Tax Liabilities	Failure to meet government reporting criteria (tax requirements, fines by government regulatory bodies)	FLSA and OSHA compliance audits, current knowledge and compliance with FICA and FUTA, minimum wage requirements, and other regulations and requirements, etc.	
☐ Business Interruption	Terrorism, destruction due to natural disaster or catastrophic weather event, illness related to contamination, sexual abuse, etc.	Business-interruption and extra-expense insurance; policies regarding refunds, contracts.	

continued on next page...

Figure 7.1

Contract Liabilities	Examples or Type	Sample Techniques to Reduce, Prevent or Control Loss	Identify Risk Control Methods and Technique(s) and Steps Taken
☐ Lease/Rental	Contracts with guest/user groups.	Agreement specifies what to transfer/what to retain. Reviewed with lawyer. OM-20,21, TR-13,14, PD-5,HW.*21-23	
☐ Employment Agreements	Agreements with staff.	Personnel policies, address at-will status.	
☐ Refunds	Camper fees, rental cancellations.	Written policy for parents/groups.	
☐ Grants	Obligations to fulfill grant stipulations.	Time line and stipulations reviewed regularly.	
☐ Sales or Purchase Orders	Limits and authority of buyers to purchase, methods of documenting orders	Guidelines specifying limits, procedures and authority to bind the corporation	
☐ Notes, Mortgage, Loans	Limits/authority to sign for camp/corporation.	Policy/controls on binding camp/corporation.	
☐ Insurance Coverage	Desired coverages, limits, exceptions, deductibles	Regular review of coverages including the general liability and umbrella liability insurance coverage. OM-11	
☐ Contracts for Service	Food service, construction, etc.	Agreements specify what to transfer/what to retain. Reviewed by lawyer.	
☐ Program Activity Contracts	Horse leasing or public stable use; rafting, community swim pool, permits for access, etc.	Agreement specifies what to transfer/what to retain and conditions of use. Reviewed by lawyer. PD-24, PC-16	
☐ Participant/user group registration	Agreement to provide services.	Waivers, releases, permission to participate, permission to treat, etc. PD-8	

Property Exposures or Liabilities:

Check all that apply to your camp

Property, Buildings and Equipment	Considerations affecting losses in this category:	Sample Techniques to Reduce, Control or Prevent Loss	Risk Control Methods and Technique(s) and Steps Taken

☐ Fire/Smoke
☐ Theft
☐ Land Movement/Earthquake
☐ Collapse
☐ Blizzard, Ice, Hail
☐ Flood
☐ Wind, Tornado, Hurricane
☐ Sewer Backup
☐ Lighting
☐ Falling Objects
☐ Vandalism
☐ Breakdown of Machinery
☐ Collision
☐ Explosion
☐ Contamination
☐ Loss of Utilities
☐ Poor Maintenance
☐ Loss of Personal Property
	• Area of the country and known risks
	• Severity of damage to your property
	• Is the building worth insuring
	• Value of items in buildings
	• Distance from emergency services
	• Seasons of site use
	• Availability of backup power
	• Cost and availability of safety equipment on sale
	• Cost and availability of insurance
	• Aging property or equipment
	• Backup systems for computerized records and documents
	• OSHA requirements
	  -Maintenance log
	  -Lockout/tagout
	  -Material Safety Data Sheets
	• Laws, codes, permits, regulations, affecting operation
		• Establish emergency plans for natural disasters OM-9/
		• Purchase property insurance OM-11.
		• Determine acceptable deductible.
		• Determine acceptable ceiling.
		• Determine what is feasible to retain (without insurance).
		• Purchase of safety, rescue, or other equipment.
		• Supervision of site when not in full use.
		• Inventories of equipment and supplies.
		• Annual safety examinations SF-4,7.
		• Assessable descriptions of electrical lines and cutoff points SF-6.
		• Train staff and participants in roles in emergency plan.
		• Establish long-term maintenance plan SF-8.
		• Hazard Communication Plan.(OSHA). Determine appropriate storage and handling of equipment, hazardous materials, and records SF-*2,11.
		• Relationship with local fire and law enforcement officials SF-3.	

Understanding legal liability and regulations

Before you get too far on your risk management planning, you should be familiar with key legal terms, regulations, and information about legal counsel.

Responsibility and liability

The greatest responsibility of organizations, owners, and administrators is the protection of the campers and staff in their care. And one of the greatest fears is a lawsuit. Let's take a look at some basic elements of responsibility and liability.

Organizations are generally liable for the wrongful acts of paid or volunteer staff. Administrators and supervisors may be liable for the negligent acts of the persons they are supervising. Even though you may have transferred the majority of risk by carrying liability insurance, your time and resources could be tied up for a long period—and your reputation affected—due to an incident even if you are found to be without fault.

In most cases an attorney appointed by your insurance company will try to settle out of court (with a settlement that will not establish or prove fault). Should an incident arise, your risk management plan will help you establish the procedures and documentation needed to protect your assets. A word of caution here, however. If procedures in your plan are not carefully followed this could be used against you. Imagine the camp that has a policy about what to do in a severe thunderstorm and the counselor didn't follow the procedures, or, even worse, didn't know the procedure.

The following are several legal terms you should be familiar with:

- In "*Loco Parentis*" or "in place of the parents" means any period that the organization or an individual assumes the rights, duties and responsibilities of the parents for a minor in their care.
- The "Doctrine of Respondeat Superior" means the organization could be held liable for the actions or nonactions of employees or volunteers when acting under the direction of the organization.
- "*Ultra Vires*" means acting outside the scope of authority or responsibility, including willful and wanton conduct or use of excessive force. In most cases the individual is charged with a criminal act. The organization may also be sued for negligent hiring or supervision.
- "Statute of Limitations" is the time in which the victim has to sue for loses. A parent may not choose to sue; however, a minor when they reach adulthood has a stated period of time that differs by state, usually three to

five years, to try to recover damages that occurred while in a camp's care. For this reason, it is important that you retain your documentation on an incident for this period of time. In cases of child abuse, there may be no limitations.

Minimizing lawsuits

Here are some tips to help minimize the likelihood of a lawsuit, or help with the defense of a claim if one is filed.

- Act quickly to give aid and follow your emergency procedures in case of an accident. The safety of the participants is your first responsibility.
- Be sure the campers, their parents, and the staff know and understand the procedures and any risks they are assuming. Some states are requiring a specific permission form for some activities; for example, horseback riding. Check with your state for specific guidelines.
- Notify your superior, legal counsel and your insurance carrier immediately.
- Try to avoid the natural feelings of being sorry or guilty that the accident happened. Be concerned, helpful, and courteous; but stay with the facts and refer questions of a legal nature to your insurance company.
- Complete an incident report documenting details of any accident or behavioral incident including location, witnesses, and sequence of events. Take pictures of the scene if possible. Do not speculate fault.
- Do not give a statement or agree to pay any bills outside of what the insurance covers without first consulting with your attorney.

In most cases the legal system is quite slow. For this reason, be sure you are documenting the incident and not depending on your memory of the situation or that of someone who is no longer employed. A good risk management plan will address identification of any situation where someone could get hurt. It also will encompass preventative actions and steps you can and should take to lessen damage in the event of an incident.

A word about regulations

There also are a number of regulations and taxes that apply to the camp industry. Federal regulations apply to all; however, state or local government regulations vary considerably.

Some states require licenses for operating a day camp; some classify day camps as day care for license purposes. Michigan, for example, requires a license for a day camp that meets their definition of camp, including operating in an outdoor environment on the same site for at least ten days.

Some states have different regulations for various types of camps; that is, for not-for-profit, religious, and for-profit camps. The first step in understanding how these will affect your operation is to secure a copy of the regulations that apply to you. It may be helpful to secure the aid of a lawyer to assist you in acquiring or interpreting the legal requirements. Your state health officials or the department of family or social services are valuable resources. For details, call your state officials, check state health-related Web sites, or network with other camp directors in the area. Here is a list of some of the questions you should ask:

- What are the permits/licenses required in your area? Which offices handle them? Is there a fee?
- What wage and salary laws affect staff salaries? What are the Occupational Safety and Health Administration (OSHA) regulations that are required for employees?
- What are the health and sanitation laws concerning sewage disposal and operation of food service including food storage, food handlers permits, dishwashing, garbage disposal, inspections, and water purity tests?
- Are background screening checks required for staff?
- Are day camp staff required to take child abuse training?
- What are special licenses required for transporting campers? Does the size of the vehicle make a difference? Do school bus laws apply to camp vehicles in your area? Is insurance required?
- Is a health center required for healthcare? What kind of certification or license is required for health-care personnel?
- Which of the following state and federal taxes are required?
  - Federal and/or state or local income tax
  - Federal and/or state unemployment tax
  - Social Security
  - Workers' compensation
  - Sales and property tax
- What are the requirements of the Americans with Disabilities Act for including persons with disabilities?

Consider an attorney

To really understand the legal lay of the land, you should, of course, consult an attorney. If your camp does not have an attorney *per se,* check with your camp partners to see if your backing organization or agency has access to legal counsel. If not, there may be an attorney who is familiar with camp operation, who might advise you *pro bono* or for a reduced fee. While an attorney is very helpful to have on your board or committee, you should understand that it could be considered "Self-Dealing" or a conflict of interest for a board member to benefit from the decisions of the board. Attorneys specialize in particular aspects of the law and a board member may be able to refer you to someone that has knowledge of the area you are interested in. It is much better to have an attorney with whom you have an established working relationship and is familiar with your operation *before* you have a crisis and you need one.

Insurance and protecting your camp

Most camps protect their operations with insurance. Ian Garner, former camp director and national director of camp and youth relations at Markel Insurance Company, emphasizes the important role insurance coverage plays in protecting a camp and its directors and officers. "Camp directors may not always be aware of all the exposures their businesses face. Working with children presents unmatched rewards, but also creates unique risks from the insurance perspective."

Garner provides an overview of camp coverage options:

Liability coverage

While good liability coverage is essential for every business, child-related businesses need specialized, high-quality protection. Children's camps need coverage that reflects their unique risks, exposures, and operations.

- **General liability** provides payment for sums you become legally obligated to pay because of damage to property of others or injuries to others that arise out of your negligence.
- **Umbrella liability** offers extra liability insurance above your primary liability and auto policies. This coverage is designed to protect you and your assets in the event of a catastrophic accident.
- **Sexual abuse liability** will protect you from allegations of sexual abuse due to negligence in your hiring, training, or supervisory practices. Defense costs should also be covered above the policy limit, which means that you will be

able to defend your reputation vigorously against these damaging assertions.

- **Child abduction liability** provides payment for reasonable and necessary expenses incurred by the camp and a child's parents following the abduction of a child from camp. Examples of covered expenses should include:
    - fees and expenses of investigative services
    - rewards leading to the recovery of the child
    - public relations and publicity costs
    - fees of independent forensic analysts
    - travel expenses and salary lost by parents during the search for a child
    - rest, rehabilitation, and psychiatric expenses for the child and immediate family members
    - medical services and hospitalization for a recovered child
- **Directors' and officers' liability** coverage provides individual protection for camp directors and officers against wrongful act lawsuits brought by customers, competitors, creditors, and others. Camp directors and officers make business decisions every day. However, if problems result from those decisions, the facility's general liability coverage may not protect these professionals. Courts continue to debate whether "detrimental management decisions" can cause injury as defined by most general liability policies. The professionals who manage a camp could find themselves defending their decisions in court.
- **Employment practices liability** protects against the threats that employers face, such as allegations of sexual harassment, wrongful termination, and employment discrimination. In this day and age, employment practices liability coverage has become more and more of a hot button for employers in all industries, especially in the social services realm.

Property coverage

- **Property coverage** covers damage to buildings, personal property, equipment, and contents caused by specific perils, such as fire, lightning, explosions, windstorms and hail, smoke, aircraft or vehicles, vandalism, and more, as named in the policy.
- **Business income insurance** covers the cost of normal business operations due to a forced shutdown of the facility. Fees lost from the unexpected shutdown of a camp because of property damage could put a significant strain on the financial resources of even the best-managed facility. The uninterrupted operation of facilities is a top priority for camp owners and that is why comprehensive and affordable property and business income coverage is so important.

Other types of coverage
- **Crime coverage** protects you against the potential dishonest acts of your employees who handle checks, money, merchandise, or equipment at the facility or in your office, as well as theft or burglary of money or securities.
- **Boiler and machinery coverage** can add protection for operations from sudden and accidental breakdowns of equipment typically excluded from property policies.
- **Commercial automobile insurance** covers owned, leased, non-owned, and hired automobiles, such as vans, pickups, and buses used at your facility.
- **Workers' compensation** is intended to pay employee medical expenses and lost wages that result from injuries sustained, arising out of, and in the course of employment at your camp. This insurance meets the employer's responsibilities as defined by state law.
- **Accident medical coverage** insures campers in your care against injuries sustained at your facility. [1]

Transportation

Just about every day camp director agrees: how you get your kids to and from camp presents one of the stickiest, hard-to-manage challenges of camp administration. If parents are dropping off their kids, you're home free. If some of your children require transportation, and providing that transportation is part of the services you're camp will be delivering, then the next section will be of interest.

In Chapter 5 you made some decisions about how your campers will arrive at camp each day. The logistics you plan for handling this vary depending on the type of transportation and the drivers you'll use. A key question you'll need to answer is: "Who has the responsibility for the transportation?" If there is a lawsuit the jury will likely decide on responsibility, and may assign some responsibility to be shared among the parties. For this reason, you'll want to have your transportation plan solidly nailed down.

Here's some general information about responsibility for varying modes of transportation.

- **Charter buses** — If the camp chartered the bus then the responsibility is shared between the camp and the charter company, and the signed agreement should specify specific responsibilities such as: maintenance, driver qualifications, licenses and regulations, supervision of campers, route, seating arrangements, insurance, etc.

- **Privately-owned/leased buses** — If the camp owns or leases the bus the camp assumes more of the responsibilities listed above.
- **Vans** — If your day camp owns or leases vans for transporting campers you should be familiar with new legislation (see inset article). The new regulations are similar to those pertaining to operations that own or lease buses.
- **Publicly-owned vehicles** — If the campers arrive on public transportation (bus, taxi, metro, etc.) the responsibility may be dependant on who arranged for the transportation but is often the responsibility of the parent who has sent the child by public transportation. The camp should specify when it assumes responsibility for the child. If the camp is using public transportation for field trips the parent should sign a permission form and the camp assumes the responsibility for supervision and for selecting a safe means for transporting campers.
- **Privately-owned vehicles** — If the camper is transported by a privately-owned vehicle the driver and/or owner assumes responsibility unless the camp has arranged a carpool, paid the owner of the vehicle, or has reimbursed him or her for expenses.

Know about the new regulations on 15-passenger vans?

The National Highway Traffic Safety Administration has issued a warning about possible roll-over hazards of passenger vans. To address the situation, the Federal Motor Carrier Safety Administration (FMCSA) adopted a new regulation defining Commercial Motor Vehicles (CMVs) in 2001. It also imposed requirements for identifying the vehicle, and maintaining safety reports. According to the new definition CMVs are defined as vehicles:

- having a gross vehicle weight rating or GVW of at least 10,001 lbs. including weight of passengers and property (baggage and equipment), or
- designed for or used to transport more than eight passengers, including the driver, that earn compensation for services. Any entity that assesses a fee, monetary or otherwise, directly or indirectly, for the transportation of passengers is operating as a for-hire carrier (CMV). This includes camps that include transportation either as a part of their camp fee or as an additional fee.

The new rule also requires motor carriers operating CMVs to file a motor carrier identification report, mark their vehicles with U.S. DOT identification numbers, and to keep an accident register. This regulation will automatically become a requirement of FMCSA one year from the date of enactment. The purpose of this regulation is to monitor the operational safety of motor carriers operating small passenger-carrying vehicles for compensation. In the same Federal Register, FMCSA published a notice of proposed rulemaking to address van operations that have been determined to pose a serious safety risk.

Courtesy of Mark Tantrum, San Jose, California

Drafting your health-care plan

An important part of your risk management plan is your health-care plan. To put your plan together, you'll need to decide the scope of care you intend to provide. Camps vary in their health-care needs depending on their clientele, type of camp, and professional medical facilities. Specific state or county regulations may also govern the level of care your camp needs to provide. Day camps are often close to medical facilities; because children go home each night, daily healthcare is often shared with the parents. As you put together your health-care plan, you should identify procedures for how people, on or off the site, can obtain routine and emergency healthcare.

The Health-care Plan Checklist in Figure 7.2 gives you a list of procedures you may want to include. A well thought-out health-care plan provides direction for meeting the health and wellness needs of campers and staff. The director, board, and/or owners should determine the overall scope of services that will be provided and establish policies. Authority for approving policies varies for each camp. Check each task when completed.

Health-care Plan Checklist

Figure 7.2

Scope and limits of healthcare provided

Health-care information on the needs of campers and staff including any special medical needs health history on campers and staff:

- health exam on campers and staff
- ratio of health-care personnel to participants
- system for evaluating the camp's ability to meet participants' needs
- permission to treat

Qualifications needed for licensed health-care provider(s), first-aid, and emergency care personnel. In addition, health professionals, (MD, RN, EMT, LPN) either on-site or accessible by phone.

Authority and responsibility of health-care administrator/manager

Authority and responsibility of program/support staff in healthcare:

- sanitation (cleanliness, hygiene, health practices in camp)

continued on next page...

Figure 7.2

- meals (nutrition, special diets, etc.)
- first aid

External medical and mental health resources access and needs: emergency, diagnostic, therapeutic

Procedures and practices —
- reviewed annually by camp and within last 3 years by physician or nurse

Health-care procedures
Procedures should be identified for how people, on or off the site, can obtain routine and emergency healthcare. There also should be procedures for communication, sanitation, and maintaining and evaluating records and services. Check when completed.

- Maintaining good health (diet, weather, exercise, rest, etc.)
- Health screening
- Eligibility for activities
- Information on each camper and staff member
- Reviewing health exams, records, and histories
- Health-care procedures for routine illness and injury care reviewed annually by physician
- Medication administration
- Preventing communicable diseases and exposure control
- Monitoring sanitation in camp
- Equipment and supplies
    - Disposal of medical waste
    - Laundering of health center linens
- First aid/CPR
    - activities and locations where first-aid- and CPR-certified staff are required and where first-aid kits are located
- Emergency assistance
- Maintaining a health-care shelter or center
    - supervision of patients

Off-site care
- Pre-trip orientation on emergency procedures and first aid
- First aid/CPR
- Health screening prior to trip
- Location of health forms

- Health and sanitation practices
- Information on each camper and staff in case of emergency
- Establishing relationships with out-of-camp providers
- Emergency transportation
- Emergency medical assistance
- Non-emergency medical assistance
- Non-emergency transportation for medical assistance

Communication and confidentiality

- Contacting parents
    - responding to parent health-care calls
    - parent information on insurance
    - follow-up after camp
- Expectations for keeping director informed on health-care issues
- Decision about persons leaving camp for health reasons
- Interaction with state, county, and local regulatory bodies
- Calling emergency assistance
- Handling media questions
- Information shared with staff

Record-keeping (seasonal and long-term)

- Individual camper and staff history and medical records
    - reviewed prior to camp
- Incident/accident reports
- Treatment records (in and out of camp care)
- Medication administered (in and out of camp)
- Insurance and billing procedures
- Sanitation records
- Parent communication log

Evaluating

- Analysis of records
- Client satisfaction

Courtesy of Tom Sawyer Camps, Pasadena, California

Developing your crisis management plan

No camp can prepare itself for every possible event. However, to provide a working understanding of what constitutes a crisis, a crisis can be defined as any negative situation that runs a risk of:

- harming human life or well-being,
- damaging camp property,
- escalating in intensity,
- falling under the close scrutiny of the news media, or
- jeopardizing the positive reputation of your camp.

When crisis hits . . . be prepared

When it comes to crisis management, two words tell you a big part of what you need to know: *Be prepared.* Crises *do* and sometimes *will* happen. No two emergency situations are alike; you have no control over when or how they will arise. All you can do is have a good plan in place to fall back on if they do. In addition to outlining the process for effectively handling an emergency, a plan also helps you keep your head when an extremely stressful situation may have scattered your judgement.

The two main areas of crisis planning are: 1) the development and implementation of emergency procedures to handle and prevent further loss or damage, and 2) crisis communications. An emergency involves danger and could pose immediate serious harm or property loss. When the danger has been eliminated and the potential for additional harm or loss to persons or property has been contained, the situation may still require crisis communications.

Make crisis preparation a priority

If your camp preparation time is limited, make your risk management and crisis planning a priority.

Drafting emergency procedures is a good place to start. While the various steps and suggestions outlined in Figure 7.3 are sample procedures and good guideposts, your own judgment about what will work in your camp should take precedent. The safety and well-being of the campers and staff ALWAYS come first.

Emergency Procedures

Figure 7.3

Major Injuries and Accidents
If you are the primary staff member at the scene in camp:

1. Count to ten and evaluate the overall situation. Do not rush or panic.
2. Take charge. Be firm and clear with your instructions to campers and staff. Use a calm tone of voice.
3. The staff member with the highest level of appropriate certification is delegated the responsibility to aid the injured party. Give priority attention to caring for the needs of the victim. The person rendering first aid must enter the information in the camp health log within 12 hours of the incident.
4. Delegate another staff member to ensure the safety of other campers by taking them away from the immediate scene and organizing singing, games, or other activities. Retain one staff member at the scene of the accident with the victim.
5. Contact the health-care supervisor as soon as possible. Provide a clear description of the emergency and your location.
6. Notify the camp director or other administrative staff in the camp office. When telephoning, if someone else answers the call, tell them: "This is an emergency, I must talk to the camp director." Do not discuss the situation with them.
7. Begin collecting the facts. What happened? How? When? Where? Witnesses? Where were the staff? Campers? What could the **victim** have done to prevent the injury?
8. Once the health-care supervisor/camp director arrives at the scene, summarize the situation and answer questions. The health-care supervisor or director will take charge.
9. Prepare accident reports within 24 hours.
10. In the case of a critical accident, serious injury, harm or fatality: Keep a responsible adult at the scene of the accident or emergency situation to see that nothing is disturbed until medical aid or law-enforcement authorities arrive.

If you are out of camp:

1. If the injury is not a life/death situation or is an illness, contact camp first. If the emergency appears to be life/death related, call 911 first (or appropriate EMS number), then notify the camp.

2. Be prepared to deal with the public and possibly the media. Indicate as pleasantly as possible that you are not authorized to speak for the camp and refer them to the camp director.

3. Do not issue any statements orally, or in writing. Do not speculate or say anything which could be interpreted as assuming or rejecting responsibility for the accident or emergency. Under NO circumstances reveal the name of the victim or other persons involved.

4. Cooperate with the public emergency personnel at the scene. Get the name, badge number, and jurisdiction of the officer taking the report. If possible, get the report number, too.

5. Do not contact the child's parents unless you have authorization from the camp director or health-care supervisor.

6. If you are a secondary staff member at the scene: Remember the camper's safety is always first!

7. Quickly and quietly follow the directions of the person in charge of the situation.

8. Do not panic . . . remember, you must set an example for the campers at the scene.

9. Offer advice to the person in charge only if you are more knowledgeable about the incident or you are asked.

10. Do not discuss or allow campers to discuss the situation with anyone other than camp personnel or law-enforcement officials.

11. Assist in preparing reports as needed.

Waterfront Emergencies

General Guidelines: In the event of an aquatic emergency, the waterfront staff member with highest qualification/position shall be in charge.

At the Pool

Near-Drowning:

1. The lifeguard signals a long blast on the whistle. This signal alerts other pool staff and watchers that it may be necessary to clear the pool and put rescue procedures into action.

continued on next page...

Figure 7.3

2. Lifeguard on duty will reach victim in the fastest possible way and administer appropriate lifesaving techniques. If she/he requires help in the rescue, she/he extends a clasped fist into the air. Remaining lifeguards assist with the rescue.

3. Lookouts and additional guards signal all campers and staff to leave the water and the pool area. The lookouts/counselors will supervise the campers.

4. One counselor will be asked to report immediately to the office and explain the nature of the incident. The health-care supervisor and camp director will be contacted immediately. If the emergency is a drowning or major injury, 911 will be contacted. (Follow procedures for Major Incidents and Accidents.)

Lost Swimmer:

If a camper is missing during a buddy check or the camper's buddy or counselor notifies the lifeguards or lookouts that a camper is missing, the following steps are taken:

1. A whistle is blown for a "buddy check." Everyone immediately gets out of the water and a recount of swimmers is immediately taken.

2. Unit staff assigned by the waterfront director or lifeguard will take other campers out of the pool area to a designated place.

3. Waterfront staff will immediately scan the pool, then check the changing room and restrooms.

4. Waterfront staff will designate a staff member to inform the camp office of emergency details. If the camper is not found, Missing Person Procedures will be followed from the Emergency Procedures Manual.

At the Lake

Capsized Canoe:

1. When the staff has spotted a capsized canoe, instruct the other campers to move away from the area. Talk to the campers and tell them to do just what they did during the "tip test."

2. If the campers are unable to maneuver themselves and the canoe to safety, a staff member should canoe next to the campers and assist them.

Lost Swimmer:

In the event that a camper has capsized his/her canoe or fallen into the lake, follow appropriate rescue techniques. If a camper is missing, follow the lost swimmer procedures for a pool, and in addition:

1. The administrative staff contacts other staff members and proceeds to the lake area with a walkie-talkie. One staff member will stay by the phone. A rescue squad (911) should be contacted, and the Emergency Procedures followed.

2. A designated drill person will stay on the shore and direct the others to look for the camper, searching with as little movement as possible. Depending on the condition of the lake, the staff may look via canoe, rowboat, or by swimming: The safety of the staff members is very important! If needed, masks, snorkels, and other rescue equipment are available at the pool area.

3. The search continues until rescue authorities arrive and take over and direct the staff on their duties.

Fire

1. When a fire is sighted, the safety of camper is the first priority. Sound the established signal (blasts of a air horn, bell, car horn, etc.).

2. Campers and staff should follow the fire drill procedures that were held within the first 24 hours of each session or as prescribed by state law.

    • Stop all activities, assemble all campers in a buddy line and count to be sure all the campers and staff are present. All persons, if possible, should have shoes on their feet.

    • Proceed quickly and quietly to the designated parking area.

    • Walk on the side of the road facing traffic. Leave room for vehicles to pass.

    • Upon arrival, do another head count and report the number of campers and staff present to the person in charge.

    • Keep the campers quiet and calm and wait for further instruction.

    • If the fire prevents you from reaching the parking area, use good judgment.

continued on next page...

Figure 7.3

- Stay put so an administrative staff can reach you OR exit quickly, using the safest route, to the nearest road. Wait at the road for assistance.
- If possible, bring the campers' medications and the unit first-aid kit.

3. Contact the camp office by intercom, walkie-talkie, or runner to let them know you've heard the signal and to receive any instructions. If a unit has not reported within five minutes, a runner will be sent to the unit.

4. If the fire is in the unit, designate one staff member to walk the campers away from the fire (upwind or downhill). Another staff member is designated to sound the signal alarm and to notify the camp office.

5. When assured the campers are safe the other staff members attempt to contain the fire using hoses, rakes, shovels, bucket brigade, and fire extinguisher. Use good judgment! Do not risk injury to staff or campers.

Missing Person Procedure

1. Upon determination that a camper is missing, determine when and where the camper was last seen. Stay calm so you don't frighten the other campers.

2. Discover (if possible) the state of mind of the camper. Was she depressed or angry, threatening to run away? Did he fall behind on a hike, or leave to visit a friend in another unit? A camper who does not wish to be found will require a wider and more careful search.

3. Do a search of the immediate area with available staff. (The camper may have wandered to the edge of the activity.) Ask nearby campers and staff if they have seen or know where the camper is. Before leaving the rest of the group to find a camper, see that they are supervised by another staff member.

4. Check any known accomplices (friends in other cabins, etc.).

5. Check bathrooms, dining hall, the cabin, and a friend's cabin.

6. Contact the camp director or other administrative personnel about the situation. Include the name of the missing camper, when and where last seen, description of child: hair, eyes, weight, height, and, as close as possible, clothing. The camp director will organize an extended search. If the camper is not

found in twenty minutes, the camper will be presumed lost. The camp director will institute a public search that will include contacting the sheriff department, camp office, and camper's parents.

7. Do not ignore the remaining campers. Be calm and positive. Acknowledge their fears and move on to some activity.

8. Complete an incident report and any other reports requested.

Intruders

1. Unfamiliar persons on the camp property may range from someone lost and looking for directions to a person with intent to do harm to persons or property.

2. Persons should be questioned to ascertain who they are and why they are here. Do not antagonize the intruder. Be polite, give assistance if possible, escort/refer the person to the camp office, or ask them to leave. Be observant as to the make, model, and license number of the car.

3. If the appearance of the unfamiliar person makes you uncomfortable, approach him/her with another staff member. Someone should stay with the campers away from the situation.

4. If the person seems threatening in any way, do not approach or take any chances. Remove yourselves and the campers from the area, notify the camp office, observe the whereabouts of the person.

5. If a child encounters an unfamiliar person, real or imagined, never tell the child that "it really wasn't anything," "there is no need to be afraid," or "it was just your imagination." Frightened children need to be allowed to experience their fear, to know that it is okay to be afraid, and to talk about their experience.

6. If you are off camp property and someone seems to be behaving suspiciously or inappropriately around your area, keep a staff member with the campers while two other staff members go to notify a law-enforcement officer or other authority.

7. Notify the camp director immediately of any intruders.

Kidnapping

1. DO NOT ALLOW ANYONE (stranger or known) TO REMOVE A CAMPER FROM CAMP!

continued on next page...

Figure 7.3

2. Escort/refer all visiting persons (stranger or known) to the director.

3. Strangers may come to the camp in search of potential victims. Custody disputes between parents can result in an attempt to remove a camper from camp. The director will verify written permission signed by legal guardian for someone to pick up a camper.

4. Should a camper be taken from camp without the expressed and direct approval of the director: Get descriptions of all persons involved if possible (hair, clothes, height, license number of car, etc.). Notify the camp director IMMEDIATELY!

Additional procedures should be established to address any weather or other natural disasters or utility failures common to your area such as earthquakes, electrical storms, tornadoes, etc. Since the 2001 terrorist attacks, many camps have added emergency procedures for terrorism and war. ACA's Web site is a good resource for a list of current procedures and resources including the Centers for Disease Control and Prevention, U.S. Department of Homeland Security, and American Academy of Pediatricians.

Courtesy of Crystal Lake Park District, Crystal Lake, Illinois

Planning for crisis management

Once the emergency is contained, move to crisis assessment. Some situations are easily identifiable as a crisis; others are not. Examining a situation against an assessment inventory can help determine the magnitude and nature of a crisis, and suggest a course of action for dealing with a situation. Let's take a look at one.

You can determine the potential organizational impact of a crisis by answering these questions:

1. Does the situation run the risk of escalating in intensity?
   - How intense might the situation become?
   - How quickly?
2. Will the situation attract the attention of the news media?
   - Will there be regional or national media coverage?
   - Will the local news media call to inquire?
3. Must we report this incident? If so to whom?
4. Are deaths or injuries to campers or staff involved?
5. Might this incident trigger a criminal or other investigation?
6. Could this situation hurt the camp's reputation and good image with our customers or the public; could customer confidence in the camp suffer?
7. Is this situation the result of something the camp did?
8. Is the camp the victim of external events or forces beyond its control?
9. Can the crisis situation by handled by on-site personnel or are other agencies, e.g. the police, needed to manage the situation?

Crisis communication

After implementing your emergency procedures, you must be prepared to communicate with parents, the media, other staff, campers and your board. To do this effectively, it is essential that you have a crisis communication plan. A crisis communication plan enables you to collect information, craft your responses, identify spokespersons, disseminate the information, and maintain a communication log to aid in any follow-up actions. A good crisis communication plan gives you a procedure for crafting messages and having them approved by the appropriate parties prior to distribution to the media. Not surprisingly, crisis communication can play a key role in shaping public opinion.

Remember: In a crisis, your camp will be measured by the speed and credibility of your reaction. For this reason, an effective crisis communication plan is essential to managing media inquiry, and protecting your camp's reputation.

Crisis communication's guiding principles

Effective and successful crisis communication is rooted in an orderly series of actions or guiding principles that give structure to crisis response. The principles below will give you a framework for assessing crisis-associated communication challenges; they also suggest some ideas that will help you meet these challenges.

- **An organized response is the best response.** A good crisis communication plan will be sufficiently flexible for use with a range of unpredictable possibilities.
- **Someone must be in charge.** As a first step, assemble a crisis communication team and designate a manager. There is no substitute for centralized control of fact gathering and information distribution.
- **Prompt communications are essential.** A sound plan may fail if action is not initiated as soon as possible. Bad news is bad news, and it must be addressed with candor and appropriate speed.
- **Allow for flexibility.** Every situation will demand some unexpected action by persons involved. Those in authority must be trusted to act according to her or his best judgment.
- **Continually test the plan.** A plan's procedures should be regularly tested against crisis simulations and updated to address any revealed shortcomings.
- **Undertake complete follow-up.** After a crisis, evaluate the effectiveness of the plan through a postmortem examination.
- **When in doubt, exceed the need.** Because events and their impact unfold quickly, those in charge should be prepared to expend effort beyond immediate need.

Forming your crisis communication team

Your crisis communication team should become active when a crisis arises, and the team should deliver timely, accurate, and balanced communications. And, as much as possible, the communications should safeguard the camp from legal vulnerability.

The crisis communications team manager may be the camp director/owner or organization administrator. The members may include board members or investors, health professionals, legal counsel, public relations, other staff or volunteers with special expertise, or community contacts.

The following is a list of questions that will help your team craft your plan for the media.

1. Who are the members of your media crisis management planning team?
2. What are your key messages to the media?
3. Who is the official spokesperson during a crisis? Have they spoken recently? Are they ready to speak today?
4. Who is the back-up spokesperson?
5. What training have they had and what additional information do they need?
6. Who has the authority to approve brief factual statements for media release and for determining when they can release them?
7. What kind of information is issued in a brief statement?
8. What kind of information is issued in a more detailed release and who has the authority to approve a more detailed media release or interview?
9. When and how is other staff informed and/or trained in their role (or non-role) in dealing with the media?
10. What experts or resources are in place and ready to manage a crisis that may capture the interest of the news media?
11. Who are the media contacts that have been established?
12. Is there a media base of operations located where there is assurance of accessible telephone lines and equipment for producing press releases?
13. How often is your plan tested and re-evaluated?

Keep in mind, even the best planning and practice includes three realities:

- The first person on the scene is not likely to be someone who has been trained to handle media relations.
- The news media may reach the scene before the legal authorities or your first available spokesperson.
- If you are not prepared to talk to reporters immediately, they will find someone who is, and that person's remarks may be how the story will break.

Crisis communication's "first principles"

- Always address a crisis situation from the standpoint of the public — not the camp's—interest. The health ands safety of your campers always comes first. Say so.
- Cooperate with the media in every possible way (within the guidelines of the communications plan).
- Be proactive whenever possible.
- Keep a running log of all media inquiries with contact names.

- Never talk "off the record."
- Use one designated spokesperson.
- Never try to explain why an accident or incident happened; don't minimize the seriousness.
- Never speculate or draw conclusions. Report only verified facts.
- Never release names of injured or deceased persons until the next of kin have been notified.

Crisis follow-up/assessment

After your incident, you'll want to:

- Gather input from the legal staff.
- Write a detailed report with complete documentation.
- Obtain photographs and/or video of the scene and secure any damaged property.
- Stabilize the situation, attend to personal needs of any victims/families; turn the situation over to proper authorities.

Be ready

No one wants to have to think about what to do if their camp has a serious, even catastrophic, incident. But consider this: Isn't it better to establish your course of action *now* rather than wait until the media is calling and parents and the authorities are at your door demanding answers?

Risk management and crisis communications plans enable you to do just that. They are important tools to keep your campers safe and your camp, its officers, and *you* protected.

Spend time on your plans. Make your plans solid and workable. Rehearse them regularly with your staff. And if, God forbid, something happens, *use them with confidence.*

[Notes]

1 Ian Garner, "Camp Insurance 101, Understanding the fundamentals of a camp insurance program" *Camping Magazine* July/August 2001.

Chapter 8

Looking Ahead to Your Future Success

There's an old saying: "Most of us spend a lot of time dreaming of the future, never realizing that a little of it arrives each day." This is as true for those of us in the day camp community as it is for everyone. At each step of the way—from program planning and development, to getting your staff together, to the first day of camp and beyond—everything you do *today* contributes to your success, not only this year, but in all future programs as well.

In day camp administration, as in most other endeavors, what really matters is how you perform over the long run. By approaching the development and implementation of your day camp program systematically, you lay solid groundwork that establishes effective and smoothly running systems that, in turn, become part of your camp's culture. That's why sitting down and trying to work through your camp's programs, administrative models, and all other aspects of your operation methodically and by the book is often the very best way of avoiding the missteps that occur in a more trial-and-error approach.

Part of this groundwork is a careful evaluation of your day camp's first year of operation (or your first year as director) before you begin to look at the future. Let's look at some of the basics of camp evaluation and benchmarking.

"How'd we do?" . . . post-camp evaluations, benchmarking and program tweaking

"How successful was this year's day camp?"

Will you be prepared to answer that question when the last camper goes home?

Camp is over, your evaluations collected. Now it's time to determine what tools you will need to measure how successful your camp was.

Think back. Remember in Chapter 1 how you thought through the purpose of your day camp and began preparing for how success would be measured in your camp? Parents, campers, funders, boards/committees, owners or supervisors may all have a different concept of success. Some will be interested in outcomes, others in safety record; some will want to know numbers or outputs such as budget or attendance figures.

For instance, is your success based on the outcomes or benefits of the experience you promised your campers? This is important information and should be included in any statements made about the success of the day camp experience. How will you know if you achieved them? What are the indicators? Will your staff know what to do and how to evaluate whether outcomes were met? How will they document the achievement? Will your success on outcomes be assessed through observation and written evaluations? If you are looking at other success factors, how will you present them? Will you need to provide an end-of-season report to a board or committee or funder? The question is: What do you and other stakeholders want to know to evaluate your success and begin planning for the future?

How will parents and campers measure success?

How will you know what your parents and campers think? Is there any difference in what they think at the end of camp and six months after camp? Remember, you only get answers for the

Tip: Pictures tell great stories about your camp's success—valuable when it comes to next year's marketing. Don't forget to take pictures. Consider giving your staff some picture-taking hints and disposable cameras. If you have a Web site, you might even want to share some pictures during camp so the parents can see their child "in action." Be sure you have secured a photo release for each child as a part of your registration process. (An example is on the sample registration form in Chapter 5.)

questions you ask. Be sure your questions are related to the desired outcomes.

Look at your outcomes and the other information you want to know from parents and draft a copy to share with committees, staff, or other camp administrators for feedback. Try to keep the evaluation short and easy for parents to fill out. Do not ask any questions or collect data that you do not intend to use.

Figure 8.1 shows a sample parent evaluation that Mary designed for Camp ARTastic. Mary sent it to parents three weeks after camp.

Administering camper evaluations

You can administer your camper evaluations in several ways. First, consider the age, reading, and writing ability of the camper. Short questions with happy or sad faces to circle may be very effective for younger campers. The evaluation may be done at the end of camp with the counselor and campers discussing the experience together. The counselor will be able to evaluate the progress of each camper better if they clearly understand the expected outcomes. Provide the counselor with guidelines for the process and a form to document camper's responses.

Keeping backers in the loop

You'll also want to let your supervisor, board, or funders know about your accomplishments. After all, they will evaluate your success in the same way that you evaluate the performance of your staff. In addition to understanding how your program reinforced your outcomes, your supervisors may want to know about how successful you were at reaching your target audience. Be prepared to answer these types of questions: Was yours the correct audience to target? Did you project realistic attendance figures? If not, why not? What about the number of returning campers? How did your plan for staffing work out? Were your cash flows and budget projections accurate? Did the site meet your expectations? What do you need to have in your database to answer these questions? Were you able to meet your income projections and did you stay within your budget?

Don't wait until camp is over to begin to gather the answers to these questions. Establish benchmarks for when you will know how you are doing and establish plans for making adjustments; in this way you can achieve or exceed your projections. Ask: "What will my funders want to know? Did I do what I said I would with the money?" Be creative, be sure to thank funders for their support, and provide them with a report that brings the camp to life for them.

Figure 8.1

Camp ARTastic Parent Evaluation

With the season barely over, we are already beginning to evaluate the success of the program to begin the planning process for next summer. We have talked with campers and staff, but your input is of the utmost importance as we begin this process. Please take a few minutes to answer the questions below. Your answers are anonymous and will be used to help improve the program and services at Camp ARTastic for next summer. We have enclosed a return envelope for your convenience.

General	Excellent	Good	Fair	Poor	N/A, don't know, or additional comments
Information received about camp prior to the season	___	___	___	___	___
The registration process	___	___	___	___	___
Communication during the session	___	___	___	___	___
Transportation to and from camp	___	___	___	___	___
Affordability	___	___	___	___	___
Camp as a safe and supportive environment	___	___	___	___	___
The site and facilities	___	___	___	___	___
The camp staff	___	___	___	___	___
Your child's counselor	___	___	___	___	___
The daily schedule	___	___	___	___	___
Effectiveness in meeting the needs of your child	___	___	___	___	___

Program Benefits	A lot	Some	A little	Not at all	N/A, don't know, or additional comment
Your child's general enthusiasm with the day camp experience	___	___	___	___	___
Expressed enjoyment of various art media	___	___	___	___	___
Showed increased ability or comfort in expressing themselves creatively	___	___	___	___	___
Excitement about projects completed	___	___	___	___	___
Demonstrated increased interest in taking care of their personal art equipment and materials	___	___	___	___	___
Willingness to share with others	___	___	___	___	___
Made friends with other children	___	___	___	___	___

How did you hear about this program? _____

Why did you choose this program for your child? _____

_____

Would you recommend this program to other parents? _____

_____

continued on next page...

Figure 8.1

Camp ARTastic is interested in serving all children in the community. Please indicate the following information about your child.

How old is your child? _____ Is your child male_____ or female_____?

The race or ethnicity of your child (optional)
_____ American Indian or Alaskan Native
_____ Asian or Pacific Islander
_____ Black or African-American
_____ Hispanic/Latino
_____ Caucasian/white
_____ Other (specify) _____

Any suggestions for improvement or concerns you might like us to know about.

Thank you for helping us provide a positive camp experience for the children in this community.

For example, if you said campers were going to increase their social skills, you might want campers to write letters to funders detailing how they made new friends as part of their camp experience. Have them communicate how skills learned in camp helped their group work together, and how the same camp-acquired skills will help them get along better in school.

If funders or your board helped you purchase equipment, take pictures of campers enjoying the equipment to send with the thank you letter.

Measuring your staff's success and evaluating how they rated the camp experience

Always strive to learn from your staff how they feel about the quality of training they received and the way camp is run. Do it early in the season—before it is too late to do anything about improving a situation. Make sure you handle any staff problems promptly. And likewise make sure your staff has the means to know if they are being successful at achieving the desired outcomes. Plan for staff meetings, individual conferences, and evaluations of both their work and yours throughout the summer. Be candid and detailed in your assessment, and keep an open and receptive mind as your staff givers you its feedback.

Finally, find creative ways of showing your appreciation for a job well done. After all, it is often the small acts of consideration that determine whether a gifted staff member returns next year.

Community relations

Remember back in Chapter 2 when you identified your target population and researched the community your day camp would serve? Following camp, it will be your duty to evaluate how your program made a contribution to that community. Craft your story carefully, and tell it well; after all, the members of that community will play a key role in getting the word out—good, bad or indifferent—about your camp.

After you have distributed flyers and asked for support, be sure to thank the members of your community for their support. But don't stop there. Get involved in the community, serve on boards and participate in community events. Share stories of camp with the local newspapers. Let the community learn who you are and how your camp makes a positive contribution to the children and families that live there.

Determining the overall success of your camp

As you reviewed the steps above you were probably thinking, "Oh, if I had only started this sooner!" Well, now is the time to think about a schedule for next year. Review the year-round schedule discussed in Chapter 5 (and which you'll find on your CD). Rearrange the dates to fit your planning cycle and add those tasks you found missing.

Planning for the future of your camp

Remember the quote that began this book? "If you don't know where you're going, how will you know when you get there?" Well, the phrase carries a special meaning as you begin to plan for your camp's future. In the same way that you can't easily find your way down a wilderness camp trail without a map, it's hard to plan your future camp program *if you don't know where you're going.*

One of the best ways to begin the process of figuring out where you're going is to put together your camp's strategic plan that outlines its future. We touched upon strategic plans in Chapter 4 during our discussion of business plans. Let's assume for a moment that you're just starting a day camp, or in a new position with an existing day camp. Your primary focus is planning for the next season. To do that effectively, you'll need a business plan.

You'll also need a strategic plan. What's the difference? For one, a strategic plan is more future-oriented. You may not have the luxury to start with a finished strategic plan; however, as you've made your way through this book you've completed research and made decisions that will help you proceed with your strategic planning. Having at least one year of experience operating the day camp and getting feedback from parents, campers, staff, and committees will also help you make some future decisions.

Strategic planning requires you to dream a little. Think about where you want your camp to be in five years. Then get to work planning ways to make that dream a reality.

A strategic plan can help you establish not only a "destination" for your camp at its five-year mark, but give you the chance to clearly define the strategy for getting there. Putting together a strategic plan also can direct your year-by-year camp planning so that what you plan and do today has a direct relevance to what you want to be accomplishing five years down the road. After you have collected all the data from your evaluations and reviewed the information with your committee and/or supervisor, take the time to look five years out, begin to lay out a plan, and "back plan" to get there. Ask: "Where should I be in years two, three, and four?"

Will Rogers probably gave us the best reason for strategic planning when the said, "Even if you are on the right track, you'll get run over if you just sit there." Don't just sit on a plan, implement it. You'll want to continue year-by-year planning to chart a vision of what success will look like in five years. Strategic planning is a journey or road map into a world of constant change; for this reason, it must be reviewed and updated periodically to remain current and enable you to keep your sights on the future while working in the present.

Strategic planning must be a team effort, and includes the stakeholders and a process for gaining agreement or commitment to the plan. The general outline for a strategic plan is pretty simple and includes three phases:

Phase 1 — Determine where you are. This will take about 10 percent of the planning group's time. The organization's mission, desired outcomes, and the research about your target audience and community completed in Chapter 2, along with your first year's evaluation, should help establish this. What is the current status, market niche, future opportunities, and weaknesses or condition after this year's season? What were our successes and failures? Why?

Phase 2 — Decide where you want to be. This phase will take about 40 to 50 percent of your group's time. The decisions made here will drive Phase 3. As a first step ask: "What is our future vision?" Reconsider the current mission and desired outcomes for participants. What would be the competitive forces? What would the areas of opportunity, areas of risk, and the critical success factors in realizing this future vision? Include such points as maintaining a positive image, secure funding, quality staff, change in leadership, and so on. Ask: "Are there critical assumptions or factors that are not typically under the organization's control that must be considered?" For example, how would a major change in the economy, war, or additional acts of terrorism, a change in the law, or additional competition affect the vision?

Phase 3 — Establish the approach and implement it. This will also take 40 to 50 percent of the planning group's time. This phase includes finalization of the strategies to realize the vision established and agreed upon in Phase 2. Establish a timeline and year-by-year benchmarks and evaluate them as needed (and revise if necessary). The timeline will include steps that may or may not be a part of the yearly operation, such as land acquisition or fund raising. Action plans, task assignments, and a system to monitor progress should be incorporated into the timeline. Remember that the commitment of stakeholders, updates on progress, and keeping excitement high are critical to the success of the strategic plan.

Use available resources and professional development tools

There is much information on available resources on ACA's Web page. Check it out periodically. Some areas of special interest are:

Camping Magazine® — If you are not a member, you will still want to read *Camping* articles. Consider that you may want to join ACA or subscribe to the magazine. If you are a member you are able to search back issues of the magazine by topic in the Knowledge Center. Information on joining ACA can be found on its Web site at www.ACAcamps.org.

ACA Professional Development Calendar — This Web page is assessable whether you are a member or not and lists workshops and courses that you may want to participate in. The Basic Camp Directors Course (BCDC) is one that may be of particular interest to you after you have at least one year's experience. The calendar is arranged by region of the country and updated frequently. Your local ACA section may have special spring training events that may be of interest to you or your staff. Regional and national conferences are also great opportunities to begin to build your day camp network.

Upcoming ACA standards courses offered by sections also will be included. These courses are held regularly to update participants on the latest standards-related information.

ACA Bookstore — A great resource for program ideas and other administrative resources.

Links with other organizations and resources — The ACA Web site Knowledge Center has listing of books, articles, other organizations and businesses sorted by fourteen area of camp management.

While you may be feeling a little overwhelmed with all the planning you have to do and the responsibility of running the day camp you are undertaking, remember that you have a unique opportunity. You are providing children with a camp experience that will, as ACA vision statement says, contribute to "Enriching lives and changing the world."

Keeping a record of accomplishments and evaluating next steps — ACA's Professional Development Portfolio is a tool to help you do just that. A copy is on the CD or you can download one from the ACA Web Site. Periodically evaluate where you are so you can make plans for further development.

Reading List

15-Passenger Van Driver Improvement Course CDs
2003, Worksafe Institute of Washington
Central Washington University

104 Activities that Build: Self Esteem, Teamwork, Communication,
*   Anger Management, Self-Discovery, & Coping Skills*
1998, Rec Room Publishing
Alanna Jones

2003 Camp Benchmarks: Program, Staffing, & Financial Profiles
2004, American Camping Association
American Camping Association

50 Ways to Use Your Noodle: Loads of Land Games with Foam
*   Noodle Toys*
1997, Learning Unlimited Publishing
Chris Cavert & Sam Sikes

Accreditation Standards for Camp Programs and Services
1998, American Camping Association
American Camping Association

Adventures in Peacemaking: Conflict Resolution Activities
1989, Project Adventure
Karl Rohnke

Bag of Tricks 2
1994, Search Publications
Jane Sanborn

Basic Camp Management 6th Edition
2004, Armand Ball & Beverly Ball
American Camping Association

The Basics of Camp Nursing
2001, American Camping Association
Linda Ebner Erceg & Myra Pravda

The Book on Raccoon Circles
2002, Learning Unlimited Publishing
Dr. Jim Cain & Dr. Tom Smith

Boredom Busters: 84 Quick Activities to Wake Up a Youth Group
1990, Group Publishing Inc.
Cindy Hansen

Bottomless Bag Again
1991, Kendall/Hunt Publishing Company
Karl Rohnke

Camp is for the Camper
2000, American Camping Association
Connie Coutellier & Kathy Henchey

Camp Clip Art CD: Volume One
2000, American Camping Association
American Camping Association

Clouds on the Clothesline: and 200 Other Games
1981, Camp Tawingo Publications
Jack Pearse

The Complete Resource Pack CD
2003, American Camping Association
American Camping Association

Crafts from Recyclables
1992, Boyds Mills Press
Colleen Van Blaricom

Creek Stompin' & Gettin' Into Nature: Environmental Activities that Foster Youth Development
2003, American Camping Association
Mary Low & Connie Coutellier

Ecology Crafts for Kids
1998, Sterling Publishing Co., Inc.
Bobbe Needham

Game On! 77 Games and Activities for Kids 5-14
2001, Human Kinetics
Pay Doyle with Michelle Harkness

Go Outside! Over 130 Activities for Outdoor Adventure
2002, Tricycle Press
Nancy Blakey

Great Kids Games
1999, Sally Milner Publishing Pty Ltd.
Lynette Silver

Health Record Log
2002, American Camping Association
American Camping Association

*Including Youth with Disabilities in Outdoor Programs: Best Practices,
    Outcomes, and Resources*
2003, Sagamore Publishing
Steve Brannan, Ann Fullerton, Joel R. Arick, Gary M. Robb, Michael
    Bender

Inclusive Games
1995, Human Kinetics
Susan Kasser

It's My Job: Job Descriptions for Over 30 Camp Jobs
1992, Edie Klein CCD
American Camping Association

Kids' Multicultural Cookbook: Food & Fun Around the World
1995, Williamson Publishing Company
Deanna Cook

The Kids Summer Games Book
1998, Kids Can Press Ltd.
Jane Drake & Ann Love

Multicultural Games
1997, Human Kinetics
Lorraine Barbarash

Outdoor Living Skills Field Guide
2002, American Camping Association
Catherine M. Scheder

Outdoor Living Skills Instructor's Manual 2002
2002, American Camping Association
American Camping Association

Outdoor Living Skills Program Manual
2002, American Camping Association
Catherine M. Scheder (based on "Take a New Bearing" by Phyllis Ford)

Parachute Games
1996, Human Kinetics
Todd Strong & Dale Lefevre

Rainy Day Games: Projects, Programs, & Play for Rainy Days
2001, American Camping Association
Michelle Carvajal Decker

Ready-to-Use Activities for Before and After School Programs
1998, The Center for Applied Research in Education
Patricia Stemmler

Super Staff SuperVision
2002, Michael Brandwein
Michael Brandwein

Team-Building Activities for Every Group
1999, Rec Room Publishing
Alanna Jones

Training Terrific Staff
1999, Michael Brandwein
Michael Brandwein

Vehicle Log
2000, American Camping Association
American Camping Association

CD-ROM Contents

Budget/Chart of Accounts (Figure 4.2/blank)
Camp Comparison Chart (Figure 2.2/blank)
Camp Daily Schedule (Figure 3.3/blank)
Camp Parent Evaluation (Figure 8.1)
Day Camp Administrative Responsibilities (Figure 5.1/blank)
Day Camp Attendance and Sign In/Out
Day Camp Business Plan (Figure 4.1/blank)
Day Camp Counselor Job Description (Figure 5.2)
Day Camp Counselor Job Description (Figure 5.2/blank)
Day Camp Director/Administrator Yearly Work Calendar/Checklist (blank)
Day Camp Director/Administrator Yearly Work Calendar/Checklist (Figure 5.4)
Day Camp Driver Records
Day Camp Group Schedule (Figure 3.5/blank)
Day Camp Master Schedule (Figure 3.6)
Day Camp Master Schedule (Figure 3.6/blank)
Day Camp Registration (Figure 5.5)
Driver Orientation
Emergency Procedures
Emergency Procedures for Drivers
Employing Minors
Health-care Plan Checklist (Figure 7.2)
Key Marketing Messages (Figure 6.1)
Marketing Strategy Chart (Figure 6.2)
Marketing Strategy Chart (Figure 6.2/blank)
Monitoring Outcomes (Figure 3.1)
Monitoring Outcomes (Figure 3.1/blank)
Most Popular Day Camp Activities (Figure 3.2/blank)
On-site Staffing Factors (Figure 5.6a)
Outcomes (Figure 1.1)
Outcomes (Figure 1.1/blank)
Planning Template for Day Camp (Figure 5.3)
Pre-Camp Training Topics (Figure 5.8)
Program Activity Operational Plan (Figure 3.7/blank)
Prospective Site Matrix (Figure 1.3)
Prospective Site Matrix (Figure 1.3/blank)
Risk Exposure Chart (Figure 7.1)
Sample Guidelines for Day Campers and the Public
Sample Permission Forms
Sample Release of Day Campers

Index